Always Leave It Better

Praise for

Always Leave It Better

"If you want to learn how to coach yourself to greater happiness and productivity, I recommend you read this inspiring memoir by Dr. Michael Prazich. Among all the authors I've worked with, he stands out in his ability to help you make the most of your life by sharing memorable parts of his own."

Steve Harrison
Quantum Leap Program for Authors and Speakers

***

"An eloquent and honestly-written reminder of how personal tragedy can lead us to our most authentic selves. *Always Leave It Better* takes you on a personal journey through Dr. Prazich's life-altering stroke and recovery, and through the divine and universal lessons that will inspire you on this shared journey of life. In respect and gratitude for a chance encounter that has left me better . . . thank you for sharing your journey, Michael."

Cindy A.T. Happe, MSW, LICSW
Rising Up Counseling, LLC, Certified Trauma-Informed Yoga Instructor, Certified Brain-Spotting Therapist

***

"Coach Mike is at his best here; weaving a story thick with wisdom and Midwestern charm. He's a person who gives all of himself, and that comes through in this book. Thanks again, Mike, for spreading your good word in this world. We appreciate it."

R. Michael Anderson, MBA, MA
Best-selling author of *Soul-Centered Leadership*

"Another person's life story and experiences can be very valuable in helping us gain insights into our own life—and *Always Leave It Better* is a great example of this. By taking us on a very intimate and personal journey through his life-threatening illness, his pain, love, fears, adventures and joys, Michael shares the lessons he learned, the importance of listening to one's inner voice, and, ultimately, the value in living as our own authentic self. He also shares the joys and rewards that come from fully living one's true path and giving to others."

Pamala Oslie
Author, Consultant, Radio Show Host, Professional Psychic Intuitive, and Aura Expert

***

"A heartwarming, humorous and, at times, hair-raising story about a mid-western kid growing up, experiencing multiple career incarnations, and eventually becoming a life-coach who imparts wisdom to people lucky enough to be his clients. This story is truly a 'hero's journey,' through which the author experiences adventure, tragedy, growth and, ultimately, redemption and peace. I recommend this for anyone seeking inspiration, as the lessons of faith and self-reliance that the author has learned (and teaches) are applicable to all of us."

KC Hildreth, MBA, MS Information Systems,
MA Spiritual Psychology
Principal, Hildreth Consulting, co-founder and former CTO and COO of GoldPocket Interactive

"Did you know there was a time before cell phones? That there were places where people actually knew their neighbors? A time when it was commonplace to encounter a person who knew how to fix a car, cook a turkey, and keep his word? In this book, and in his own quirky style, Michael shares some nuggets about days gone by, and days yet to come. Whether you're a devout theologian, an atheist or a spiritualist, *Always Leave It Better* offers some timeless advice on approaching life. So put down your cell phone, grab a cup of coffee or a savory cocktail, and let Michael share his journey."

Jeff D. Berk, MBA, PhD
Purple Mountain Investment Advisors, LLC

***

"This book describes Michael's life journey and is full of discoveries that have become the foundation of his mature and enlightened view of the world. He speaks to all of us who have felt the seemingly inexplicable connection between distant friends. Ever had the phone ring and say, 'I was just thinking about you, how nice that you called'? Michael's story is filled with these moments, only on a much deeper level. Guided by his own life experiences, and by listening intently to the quiet voice from within, Michael finds his path to a more meaningful, balanced and healthy mind/body connection. Michael's lessons are practical, tangible and inspiring."

Harold (hod) Dahl, CPA
Chief Quality Officer, CliftonLarsonAllen LLP

Always Leave It Better

One man's journey through life,
and lessons learned along the way

By Dr. Michael Prazich

PERFECT LOOP
coaching
THE BEST IS YET TO COME

Always Leave it Better

Perfect Loop Coaching
9653 E Pershing Ave
Scottsdale, AZ 85260
Phone: 612-568-LOOP (5667)

Contact the Author: bookernmike@gmail.com

Cover Design by Daria Brennan (beegraphica.com)
Author Photograph by J.D. Berk
Editing by Chris Nelson

ISBN-13: 978-1544167824

Library of Congress Control Number: 2017903822
CreateSpace Independent Publishing Platform, North Charleston, SC

Thank You

Personally, I don't believe in coincidences. If our paths have crossed sometime in this lifetime, it was for a reason. And, if I'm fortunate enough to have you call me your friend, I am blessed. In some way, you have been an integral part of my journey and have helped guide it. Thank you for your time, your friendship and your guidance.

~

I lovingly dedicate this book to:

My beautiful sisters, Posie and Toot

My beautiful nieces, Courtney, Alexis and Kalison

My beautiful grandniece, Melayna

My parents, Nick and X—may they know their kids and family are doing well, and we miss you

. . . and my companion and the most "beautiful boy" in the world, Booker.

Michael

Contents

Always Leave It Better

Preface

What's happening?

Why does the ocean water look a different shade of blue than it did when I started my windsurfing lesson?

I'm looking straight ahead . . . and I'm seeing double . . . Everything is shaking side-to-side. I hear my instructor, Brian, yelling, but I can't make out his words.

What is happening?

I've never had a headache before, but now it feels like someone is pounding on the back of my head with a hammer. I lie down on my board and wrap my arms around it so I won't fall off. Brian paddles over to me and I hear him asking what's wrong . . . *but I can't lift my head to answer him.*

Brian waves his arms and I hear the sound of an outboard motor drawing close and stopping. I feel myself being lifted into the boat—but why can't I use my right arm to help them?

I'm feeling nauseous and getting sick to my stomach.

Brian and the boat driver take me to shore and call 911. Soon I hear the voice of an ambulance driver telling me I'll be okay. He asks my name and I struggle against the beating on the back of my head and the dry heaves rising from my stomach to answer . . . but I fail, and the driver must see the fear in my eyes, because he doesn't ask me again.

***

The next thing I remember is waking up on a small bed with a blood pressure cuff on my left arm. My bed is encircled by a privacy curtain. A friendly female nurse's face looks down at me and says,

"Hi, Doctor. You're in the emergency room and your doctor will be here shortly. Don't try to talk." She hands me a pen. "Please sign this consent-to-treatment form."

Through my double vision I take the pen as she holds up the clipboard with the form and points to the line next to a yellow "X."

I lower the pen towards the form . . . but I can't get anywhere near the piece of paper, much less the yellow "X." I feel a frightening disconnection from my body and fear surges through me.

She gently guides my hand to the clipboard and softly says, "Just make an X, if you can. You're doing fine."

I do my best, all the while thinking to myself, "Can't they do something about that damn hammer beating on the back of my head?"

***

"Hello, I'm Dr. Simons. I'm a neurologist." I look up and see a tall, thin man looking down at me, approximately my age and with a receding hairline. A slight but encouraging smile lies beneath his thin mustache. The pain in the back of my head has become a dull ache now. "Could you please put both arms straight out to your sides, then touch the tip of your nose with the forefinger of each hand?"

This sounds like a simple enough request.

With my left hand I can easily touch my nose . . . but when I try with my right hand I can't even hit my *head* with my finger.

The same fear I'd experienced in the ambulance grips me all over again. What is *wrong* with me? Why is my body failing me? And the back of my head is throbbing again.

He says, "I'm going to order a spinal tap ASAP to see if there's any blood in your spinal fluid."

Spinal tap? That sounds painful. And why my *spine*? My mind is now swimming all over with the worst case scenarios of not ever being able to use my right arm again or, even worse, of being paralyzed for the rest of my life.

A young, right-handed dentist with no right side! Now I'm real scared, and I'm sure the fear shows in my eyes, because they're filled with tears.

To be continued . . .

PART 1

THE JOURNEY OF A BOY TO A MAN

"Happiness cannot be traveled to, owned, worn or consumed. Happiness is the spiritual experience of living every minute with love, grace and gratitude."

~ Denis Waitley

A Perfect Life?

"Afoot and lighthearted I take to the open road,
healthy, free, the world before me."

~ Walt Whitman

"Begin, be bold, and venture to be wise."

~ Horace

"Have you ever thought what it would be like to grow up with a perfect life?"

I was having a beer with Joe, an Army buddy, and I added, "If I were to raise a son, Joe, I'd like to raise him exactly the same way I was raised. But I don't think that's possible today."

"Why do you say that?"

I explained how I grew up in northern Minnesota, in an area known as the Mesabi Iron Range. It was a forty to forty-five mile stretch of two-lane highway connecting fifteen to eighteen small towns whose residents were made up of eastern European or

Scandinavian decedents. Many were first or second generation Europeans who had immigrated to the United States to find their dreams. Since the area had one of the richest iron ore deposits in the world, they settled on "the Range" to start their new lives working as unskilled laborers in the surrounding mines and businesses.

Good education for their children was a priority for the immigrant citizens, and since the mining companies paid significant amounts of state taxes, some of the big winners in the area were the school systems. My high school had a total enrollment of less than six hundred students. The school, built in 1920, had marble hallways, an Olympic-sized marble swimming pool, metal and woodworking shops, home economic rooms, and an auditorium with striking murals, velvet curtains and padded chairs. It was also surrounded by beautiful, well-tended grounds. My teachers were some of the highest paid high school instructors in the country. Overall, the school system was so good that some families even moved to the area from other states to enroll their children.

Two of my classmates and I went all the way through junior high, high school, junior college and dental school together. Another three of my classmates became physicians, two became attorneys, three became successful CEO's and many others became successful teachers, therapists and engineers. In short, we received an excellent education, and we took advantage of it.

My youngest sister, Toot, was born when I was ten years old, and she was a true blessing to our family, especially my mom and dad. I have wonderful memories of pushing her stroller down the main street of our little town and how everyone we passed on the sidewalk stopped to comment on how beautiful a little girl she was. Toot and my other sister, Posie, were the apples of my father's eye. As there were nine years between them, Toot could almost be considered an only child, and we all loved treating her as one.

My family lived behind the office area of my father's business. Our living quarters were made up of three small bedrooms, one bathroom, a living room, a dining room and a kitchen built over a garage that could accommodate my father's work truck and our family car, when one was parked behind the other. Our space was compact, but warmth and welcome were omnipresent in the atmosphere. Everyone—my sisters, our friends and strangers alike—loved to visit our family home because "X" (my mother's name was Xenia) always had the coffee pot on, cold milk in the refrigerator and the toaster plugged in and ready to accept two pieces of Vienna bread that would come out golden brown, just asking for butter or homemade jelly. More often than not, mom had a joke or two to tell (sometimes they were a little "blue"), and she loved to hear about her guests' current situations. If they wanted to share problems, she always had a loving ear to lend. To this day, my sisters and I smile as we recall how our friends stopped by to visit X even when we were away at college.

Strangely, she very seldom ate the toast she so lovingly served. X was an excellent baker and cook, but she was always bothered with indigestion. She seldom ate an entire meal, but instead grazed throughout the day. We believe now that she was gluten-sensitive before it was "cool" and, sadly, before she could have known how to alter her diet to be more comfortable.

Growing Up

*"One of the luckiest things that can happen to you in
life is, I think, to have a happy childhood."*

~ Agatha Christie

As soon as I was old enough to ride a bike I gained my freedom. In the summer my friends and I would meet and either go swimming, play baseball, shoot baskets, go fishing, build forts, explore the woods or do all the other things boys do. The only rule I had was to be home for supper. But, being a growing boy—and hungry most of the time—I frequently made excuses to my buddies and went home for lunch, too. Bicycle helmets weren't mandatory because they hadn't been invented yet. Sunscreen was rarely important. To make my bicycle sound "fast" I used clothespins to attach baseball cards to the spokes. And of course I had to chew the sugar-laden bubble gum that came with the cards.

There were twenty-one first cousins in my family. A number of us were within three years of age of each other. I treasured growing up with so many cousins. My aunts and uncles formed a close-knit group, so there always seemed to be family gatherings. All of us nieces and nephews were on our own having fun and, as might be expected, much of the time was filled with mischief. The younger boys (myself included) looked up to and tried to emulate our older cousins. We rolled up the sleeves of our short-sleeve shirts, acted "cool," and tried to wear ducktails in the back of our hair like they did. But, because most of us wore our hair short, the ducktails looked more like bad hair days than the hairdos of the Everly Brothers—the cool-looking singers popular in my high school days. We also tried smoking cigarettes. Some cousins, both male and female, continued smoking into adulthood, but most of us quit after throwing up the first time we tried to inhale the unfiltered Camel cigarettes.

Teen night dances were common and roller skating parties filled my summer weekends. These events were my first exposures to testosterone-filled teenaged boys wanting to impress cute teenaged girls. Like my father, I wasn't a large person and, while in middle school, I was confronted several times by larger kids. The first couple of times I tried to walk away, but my attempts to avoid contact weren't respected by the larger boys and I took a couple of whippings. When I got home after the second confrontation, my father suggested a simple way to gain respect: "Never start a fight, but never back down, and always get in the first two or three punches."

I got into my first two fistfights at a roller rink and at a county fair—both over girls—and to my surprise I realized I was fearless. I didn't worry about getting hurt and I actually liked the challenges. My father's shared experiences of boxing paid great dividends to his only son.

I went to all of my high school proms and even to a couple of proms at neighboring high schools. I had a healthy, happy and fun-filled high school social life. Even though I grew up in the time known as the age of sex, drugs and rock 'n' roll, I was sexually inactive until I was nineteen years old. When that status changed, a whole new world opened up and I became what I was: a healthy, virile young man.

I felt blessed to grow up with two loving parents. They supported their children in everything we did, such as school activities and, in my case, athletics. If I'm correct, none of my high school friends came from divorced/single parent families; in fact, I don't recall anyone in the school coming from broken families. This, of course, is far less common today, and I believe it contributed to our general feeling growing up that "all is well," and made all of us feel more grounded as we grew up. I truly wish that dynamic was the norm today.

There were other differences, too, of course. Another example of how times have changed is that, back then, if a high school athlete was caught smoking or drinking beer, they would be ruled ineligible to play all sports for one year; there was a zero tolerance policy for that kind of behavior. Another big difference was that if a girl got pregnant in high school she usually moved out of town to have the baby. She might later return to resume her classes, or she might instead enroll in a different high school. The teenaged father usually moved to another school to continue his education.

Oddly enough, in spite of my fairly normal—if lively—early years, I always knew I was different from my friends and cousins. Many of my high school classmates and cousins married their high school sweethearts, started families and then chose and became successful in varying professions. But from the eighth grade—age fourteen or so—I knew I wanted to be a dentist. I also knew I wasn't going to marry a high school sweetheart and stay in northern Minnesota. I didn't know exactly where I would end up living, but I pictured a small mountain town that had four seasons and a college.

Funny how life works out sometimes . . .

Richie

"He who loses wealth loses much;
but he who loses a friend loses more. "

~ *Miguel de Cervantes*

I grew up in a consolidated school district, which meant a large group of students from the nine small towns that made up our district were bussed to school daily. Each town had their own elementary school, but only one town had the middle school, and the largest town out of the nine was where the high school was located. We started meeting friends from the other little towns in middle school.

Both sets of my grandparents came to the United States from Yugoslavia through Ellis Island and settled in northern Minnesota. (I'm proud to say at one time I could read, write, understand and speak Serbo-Croatian fluently, but like anything else, "If you don't use it, you lose it.") The religion I was raised in was Serbian Eastern Orthodox, and the nearest Serbian church was thirty miles from my house, so many of us kids rode a bus to church every Sunday for Sunday school and church services. The bus stopped at each small town. Four of us mischievous boys—Richie, John, Danny and I—would occasionally skip Sunday school and church and go to a little bar/convenience store to play the pinball machines and listen to the jukebox. We would be sure to make it back to catch the bus home. (I swore my sister to secrecy.) The four of us would get to know each other better as we entered middle school and went on through high school together.

Growing up was a carefree time for me, but as I entered high school, the military draft was in full force and drafting eighteen- and nineteen-year-old boys, at least those who were not enrolled in college. Many were sent to Vietnam.

My first exposure to a particularly painful sadness came on the day I learned that one of my closest high school friends, Richie, had been killed on his last day in Viet Nam. He had been coming off guard duty when a U.S. soldier—on his first day of active duty—panicked and shot at what he thought was enemy movement.

I loved Richie as the brother I never had; he was like family to me and his loss really hit me hard. I was one of the pallbearers at his funeral—the first I had attended as an adult—and I was struck by the outpouring of sympathy and love offered to his family by our community. What's more, I talked with the two soldiers who accompanied Richie's body home. There had been times when they'd returned the remains of soldiers to loved ones and had been beaten or had their lives threatened. By contrast, they told me they'd never been treated as well as they were being treated by the people in our town. Richie's parents in particular had insisted on putting them up in the nicest motel available (rather than the dingy one they had been scheduled to stay in). They were included in meals and other activities as well. In other words, they were made to feel welcome at a time when our country was divided about the war and tensions ran high. This, I believe, speaks volumes about the warmth of the community in which I grew up.

Richie had apparently had a premonition and, in a letter addressed to his parents the day before he was killed, he told them that if something were to happen to him before he returned home, they should take the money he had saved and sent home and use it to throw a big party to celebrate his life—and not mourn his death. An excerpt from his letter reads:

> *I thank God each night for the happiness I've had in the past. If He should take me tomorrow, He's already given me more than so many will ever have. I'm in* love *with* life.
> *Richie*

It was a powerful time for me and for our community. There was grief at losing Richie, but there was also a tremendous expression of love and gratitude coming from both the community and from Richie's family.

What's more, the loss of my very dear friend brought home to me a clear sense of the fragility of life.

I didn't realize it until later, but these emotions coalesced to form the cornerstones not only of my later coaching work, but also of my personal approach to life.

When I later tried to distill the essence of these feeling and thoughts into words, I came up with the following, which has for many years been the signature to my personal emails:

> *Yesterday is a canceled check,*
> *Tomorrow is a post-dated check,*
> *Live today and always Love.*

Those sixteen words state my philosophy of life. And I have Richie to thank for helping me find them.

Parents

"One of the biggest blessings in the world is to have parents to call mom and dad."

~ Jim DeMint

Nick

My father, Nick, was a short and wiry but powerful man who boxed for sport in his younger days. His beautiful, light blue eyes complimented his easy demeanor and quiet but fun personality. He was the oldest of four sons and, due to the early death of his father and the confinement to a hospital of his mother, he had spent many of his younger years taking care of three of his brothers. One of his brothers died rather early in his adult life, and when the other two reached their ages of independence, he enlisted in the military, spent nine and a half years in the Army Air Force and planned to make the military a career.

But life had different plans for him. He fell in love with a lady named Xenia and they had two children: first me, and then, a year and a half later, my sister, Posie. Dad retired from the military and we moved from Colorado Springs to northern Minnesota in order to be closer to mom's six brothers and sisters and their families. Dad went through the licensing channels to become a master plumber (plumber's helper, apprentice, master plumber) and after achieving the Master Plumber certification he moved our family to a small town twenty-five miles away and started his own business.

Dad was an excellent plumber and craftsman. As the ultimate do-it-yourselfer, he could rebuild a car engine, wire a home or fix any small engine. He took a lot of pride in his plumbing work and never failed to come to the aid of anyone who called, day or night, with a plumbing problem. He often did favors for people who needed help, sometimes without compensation. A plumber in a small town in northern Minnesota didn't command—or demand— the service call fees, travel fees or "off-hour" charges so often seen in today's world. He was a perfectionist and was very methodical in his work and life. He didn't respect shoddy work that was done hurriedly and I remember him saying to me, "The more you hurry, Michael, the less time you'll have." I'm sure he was referring to having to redo something.

If I visited the homes of friends and, for some reason, ended up in the basement, I could tell when my father had done their plumbing. His jobs had no solder visible at the copper joints. The pipes were hidden whenever possible; one could tell that care and thought had been used in their placement.

My dad and I had a typical father/teenage son relationship. For the most part, I stayed out of trouble, but when I pushed the envelope of independence—as most teenaged boys do—he and I would verbally spar about misunderstandings. But never was there any physical punishment, either from my mother or father. This wasn't the case for some of my cousins, so even at a young age my sisters and I were aware of and grateful for the way our parents handed out punishment.

At one time my dad was approached by the State of Minnesota to be the state plumbing inspector for northern Minnesota, but he turned the offer down because it would mean there would be times when he wouldn't be home for his family. Family was his priority. He had put three kids through college and was supportive of us at every event in which we participated.

So I was a little surprised when, before he passed, he shared with me the one thing he was very sorry about: he was sorry he had never taken his family on a vacation. I took his hand, looked into his blue eyes and told him not to worry about it and that we had forgiven him a long time ago. I also told him we all learned both a tremendous work ethic from him as well as the importance of enjoying our families. His smile lit up the room and, for the first time in my life, we each had tears running down our cheeks at the same time.

Dad was respected by everyone in his profession as well as the people he had served. His word was gold, and he could be counted on to do whatever he said he would. As stated earlier, I not only adopted an excellent work ethic from him—I also learned to enjoy life. Many of his sayings resonate in my mind to this day:

Always leave everything better than you found it.

You're only as good as your word.

Always do the best you can in anything you do.

Be proud of your heritage.

Respect your elders.

Honor our military personnel.

A few words on this last one: I remember how proud my Dad was when I told him I was joining the Army. His military service meant the world to him. I'm very proud to say I'm a deeply patriotic veteran.

To me and to my coaching clients, these are simple but timeless ways to live, and when put into action, priceless.

Xenia ("X")

It is often said daughters are closer to their fathers and sons are closer to their mothers. Maybe it's that males are programmed to be the protectors of the females in their lives. Regardless, this was definitely the case between X and me. I think maybe she and I had somehow been together in a previous life. We communicated very well—better than my father and I did. She always seemed to understand me, and she knew I would be leaving after I graduated from dental school. She never pressured me by asking when I was going to get married and settle down, and she always welcomed the women I brought home to meet my parents. And, to a person, they loved her, too.

Prior to my folks getting married, X worked for Bell Telephone. After I was born, she was a stay-at-home mom. Consequently, all three of her children were the beneficiaries of Nick and X's joint decision for her to be a "domestic professional."

Stay-at-home mothers were much more the norm than the exception when I was growing up. In fact, I feel that the trend of mothers being domestic professionals was a major factor in the productivity of the baby boomer generation. I also believe that the now common disruption of family units through divorce—and the resulting need for the moms of the X and Y generations to enter the workforce—are major reasons for the delinquency problems of young adults over the last three decades. There is tremendous value in a home that has the love, mentorship and discipline found in a loving, two-parent family unit. As I have said above, I feel incredibly blessed that I grew up in such a home.

When Dad transitioned at 88, mom, then 85, went into an assisted-living facility conveniently located between my sisters and me. The three of us decided mom should see at least one of us daily and, since both of my sisters worked full time and I had flexibility in my schedule, I was able to spend the better part of the work week with her. She loved it when her son "the dentist" (as she introduced me) came to take her to lunch in the community banquet room. I would always arrive early so I could fix her hair first, and then we would walk together to the banquet room. I would stay after lunch or dinner to tidy up her apartment and talk with her. Her memory was always very sharp and I learned more about her family's early years in those short talks than I had ever known before. Even though she had macular degeneration, she tried very hard to be independent.

I filled her pill boxes weekly and my sisters and I would later find the pills that mysteriously missed her mouth under her small kitchen table. We also found the used dental floss she thought she had thrown away, but which was now wrapped around the wheels of her walker. We placed bright orange tape around two buttons on the microwave in her apartment: one around the "one minute" button and the other around the "start" button.

Many times (and without her trying) X's actions resulted in humorous events, now wonderful memories. She would be the first one to laugh at herself and would often say or do something that made everyone around her laugh.

There were times when she knew which buttons to push to get under my skin, too. I remember her sitting in the passenger seat of my car while I was driving us in a blizzard on slippery roads. She liked country music so we were listening to a country station. I had both hands on the wheel and was trying to focus through horizontally blowing snow while correcting the slipping and sliding of the tires on the slippery road.

She said she didn't like the song that was on the radio.

I said curtly, "It'll be over in a couple of minutes," and continued focusing.

She said again that she didn't like the song.

Nervous and irritated, I made the cardinal sin of taking one hand off the wheel to change the station on the radio. The car hit an icy patch and immediately started spinning out of control down the road. I remember the car making at least two full circles as we headed towards a snow-filled ditch.

The words that came out of her mouth as we were spinning?

"Oh, shit, here I go!"

Snow billowed up over the car as we hit the ditch and I looked over at her and saw her shaking her head back and forth like it was my fault. Within a minute there was a knock on my window; a man in a large SUV had been following us, had seen us pirouette down the highway and attempt to make a snow fort in the ditch. He had a tow rope, which he hooked on my car, and then he pulled us back onto the road.

When it was over I looked over at X, she looked at me, and we started laughing. She had periodic episodes of incontinence, and the laughter triggered one of them. Thank goodness for Depends and leather interiors.

For the final two-and-a-half years of her life I felt our roles were reversed: mom was my child and I was her protector. Xenia was a true angel. I still use her microwave, but I've taken off the bright orange tape. Pictures of her and my father's smiling faces are strategically placed around my home, and the homes of their daughters.

***

If I could do one thing to better mankind it would be to have children grow up in a two-parent, functional family. The impact the union of my parents had on my life and the lives of my sisters is something profound and empowering that I carry with me to this day. It has grounded me and given me a sense of security from which to launch my own adventures.

Dentistry

"The first duty of a human being is to assume the right functional relationships to society—more briefly to find your real job, and do it."

~ Charlotte Perkins Gillman

I decided on dentistry as my profession in the eighth grade. My youthful choice was primarily based on the influence of two men in my life: my father and my dentist, Dr. Bill Hudelson.

Dad taught me how important it was to treat people well, and he encouraged me to follow my dreams.

Dr. Hudelson taught me how to be a good dentist *and* a good person.

My first dentist—pre-Bill Hudelson—had been a sober-faced man who always wore the same tie. His two nurses were always dressed in white. The air in his office was permeated with the cloying smell of camphor and there was never any music playing.

24

The only sound I remember was the high-pitched screech of the dental drill.

Dr. Hudelson was different. I could tell he tremendously enjoyed being a dentist. The atmosphere in his office was light and friendly. Fun music piped into every room, and everything reflected happiness. His entire staff always seemed to be smiling. They dressed in pastel colors and seemed to enjoy working as a team and helping each other.

Bill was also a pilot. He had his own plane, and he and another dentist owned a cabin in Canada to which they would often fly to go fishing. He and his wife had five children—three boys and two girls—and they did a lot as a family.

This whole picture of Bill—his office, his plane and the freedom to fly to another country with a friend to fish—appealed to me.

The strange things that make an impression on a fourteen-year-old boy . . .

Fast forward several years: while in community college at age nineteen I was accepted into dental school. As previously mentioned, this was a time when the Viet Nam War was ongoing. The military draft was in place, but individuals who were enrolled in college were draft exempt.

At first I was only conditionally accepted into dental school, which means I was placed on a waiting list and, if someone declined their acceptance, I would be given the opportunity to enroll. I had only applied to one school.

I often wonder what my life would have been like if I hadn't been accepted into dental school. I carried a low draft number, and I would no doubt have been drafted into the military immediately and sent to Viet Nam with my other high school classmates who weren't enrolled in college.

Evidently, there was a bigger plan for me.

When I got into dental school I realized something else about Dr. Hudelson. Not only was he a warm and friendly dentist, he was also an immensely skilled practitioner. He had been asked to be a clinical instructor at my dental school, and he would fly down to Minneapolis every two weeks to teach dental students. Over the course of the two years I was in school, he and I became good friends.

After graduation I had three months before I was to report to my Army duty post in Oklahoma. Bill invited me to work in his office until I left. My relationship with him had transformed from that of a boy idolizing his childhood dentist, to a student respecting and learning from a mentor's technical excellence, to having a big brother/buddy with whom I worked. I even dated his daughter for a while, and he took me to Canada to go fishing. Bill Hudelson died of a massive stroke at age fifty-two.

Theta

"If you always attach positive emotions to the things you want, and never attach negative emotions to the things you don't, then that which you desire most will invariably come your way."

~ *Matt D. Miller*

I entered dental school with Dillon, a good friend and high school classmate. When we left our small towns on the Mesabi Iron Range and moved to the big city of Minneapolis we were like fish out of water. We had never been exposed to the vast number of students at a large university—not to mention the very concepts of heavy traffic and irritating things like having to search for parking and getting parking tickets. I think we were perfect examples of the adage, "You can take the boy out of the country but you can't take the country out of the boy."

Our freshman year we shared a small, third-floor room at the Delta Sigma Delta dental fraternity house located only blocks away from the dental school. We put our construction skills to good use and maximized all of the space in the small room, building in a desk as well as some shelving for clothes and books. We even wired a light above the desk. The house itself had been built in the early 1900's, and it already had many stories to tell before we added our own to it. Thankfully, walls can't talk.

During the four years I spent in school, the resident family of "Theta Chapter" was made up entirely of dental school students. They were from different towns and states, and they were all males. We had a hired cook, a dental laboratory in the basement, and an elected house manager. Each of us was assigned house duties, and elections for leadership positions were held annually.

Everyone's classes ran from eight to five, Monday through Friday, and the mandatory dress code was shirt-and-tie. This rigorous school schedule resulted in rigorous afterschool playtime. At that time Theta Chapter was known for having three things: excellent intramural sports teams, some of the top students in each dental class, and the best parties on the University of Minnesota campus. It was customary to go through ten to twelve sixteen-gallon kegs and six to eight eight-gallon kegs of beer at each party. Every female nursing, dental hygiene, and physical therapy student as well as the entire dental school were invited to the parties. The beer was usually gone in the first two to three hours, with much of it being spilled on the dance floor (the living room sans the furniture, which was moved outside). Visits from the University Boys in Blue were common and they'd always leave asking us to keep the noise down to a roar.

Truthfully, the popular movie *Animal House*, which was set around the same time, had nothing on the Theta Chapter parties, which were known as "Hoggers."

I was one of the younger members of my freshman class, and the competition for grades, was intense. Over 50 percent of my classmates had their bachelor degrees and a couple of them had their masters degrees. I only had a two-year Associate Degree from a community college. Up to this point school had come fairly easily to me; I had never received anything lower than a B.

At that time the University of Minnesota was on a quarterly system. During in the first quarter I started shirking my studies and spending time with upper classmen relaxing, watching television and drinking beer. I'm sure I thought to myself, "This isn't too bad."

I'll never forget going home for the first quarter break. It was great to be home, away from the hustle and bustle of the city and the demands of school. I was home for about a week when early one morning I heard my mother's voice call to me.

"Michael, wake up and get out here." She did not sound happy.

My quarterly grade reports had been sent to my parents' address and she had opened the envelope. The report was unfolded and sitting in the middle of the kitchen table.

There in black and white next to the class "Oral Histology" was my grade: a big fat **D**.

I went from never getting a C to getting three C's, one B and one D. Because of this I was on probation the second quarter. I changed my priorities and started studying and spending free time catching up. I got off probation after the second quarter but only with the lingering taste of humility and challenge.

***

Theta Chapter still has Hoggers, but **with time comes change.** These days half of every dental class is made up of women, and with females living in the house and sharing duties equally with males I'm sure the "testosterone zone" is much smaller and the atmosphere has changed for the better. No doubt the parties are still a lot of fun, but tamer and safer. The mandatory shirt-and-tie dress code was abolished after my third year and medical scrubs were and still are the dress of the day.[1]

---

[1] The fraternity, Delta Sigma Delta, is still going strong too, and it has also become more inclusive over the years. Founded in 1891, it's currently the only international dental fraternity. It has thirty-three undergraduate chapters and forty-two alumni chapters in the United States, England, Australia, New Zealand, and more.

Finding My Tribe

"It's the little details that are vital. Little things
make big things happen."

~ John Wooden

I loved being a dentist. It was my profession *and* my hobby, and perhaps because of this I became a very good dentist. After my two-year commitment to the Army was completed, I purchased a very well-established practice in Flagstaff, Arizona.

How I found the practice is a good story.

While in the Army, I took a military leave of absence to go to Arizona and take the Arizona State Dental Board examination. The board exams were given once a year and, out of all the states in the U.S., Arizona had one of the highest failure rates for first-time participants. The two-day clinical exams were given in Florence, in the Arizona Maximum Security Prison; the patients used for the proficiency practical exams were inmates.

When I took the test, the temperature was 114 degrees and

there was no air conditioning.

I was confident in my dental abilities, but I wanted to minimize any subjective reasons the examiners might have to justify their high failure rates. So it certainly didn't hurt my chances for passing that I brought a six-foot circulating fan into the clinic and strategically placed it in front of my dental chair. Strangely enough, the board examiners seemed to find a way to congregate around me, and so were able to see the quality of my work.

I passed the exam and was even asked to complete dental procedures on two patients whose out-of-state dentists chose, because of the heat, not to return for the afternoon session to complete the procedures they had started that morning.

When the exam was completed I took a drive up to Flagstaff, Arizona.

I fell in love with Flagstaff immediately. I had visualized myself practicing in a town with a few specific criteria, namely one that had a university, was close to snow skiing and hiking, had four seasons to enjoy and was close to warm weather. Flagstaff met all of these criteria. Even though I had a couple of wonderful opportunities to return to Minnesota, I was reluctant to move back to the harsh winters. I visited four dental offices in Flagstaff, met the dentists, and left a resume with each one. I told them I was planning on moving to Flagstaff and that, if they were looking to sell their practice or add an associate, I would welcome the opportunity to talk with them.

When I returned to my duty post in Oklahoma I wrote a letter to each of the four dentists thanking them for taking the time out of their busy schedules to meet with me. This ended up serving me well. One of the dentists, Dr. Rollin Gosney, kept the letter under the blotter on his desk and one day after he and his family decided to move back to northern California, he called me. Dr. Gosney explained that since I had done him the courtesy of writing the thank-you letter, he wanted to give me the first option to buy his practice before advertising it for sale.

I purchased the practice and, just like that, I was scheduled to treat patients three months before I even moved to Flagstaff.

***

Lesson: Sometimes a simple written "thank you" pays big dividends. In this age of emails and little face-to-face communication, a personal note is nice.

Work Can Be Fun

"It is nice finding the place where you can just go and relax."

~ *Moises Arias*

As I mentioned, dentistry was more than just a job to me. I enjoyed it immensely and was, in fact, a perpetual dental student. The Army had provided some excellent dental experiences, and some of the treatments I learned there were unique to Flagstaff. What's more, even after I had completed my training I enrolled in an average of 180 hours of continuing education each year, despite the fact that Arizona only required fifteen hours per year to maintain a current dental license. I gained a reputation for keeping abreast of the latest developments in dentistry, and this in turn attracted many new patients, some from hundreds of miles away.

Like Dr. Hudelson, I loved my profession.

When I arrived in Flagstaff there were twelve dental offices. All of the newer dentists, including me, had replaced a dentist who had either retired or passed away. All twelve of us had busy practices and the relationships between us were very cordial. We didn't feel as if we were in competition with each other. Although different in philosophies, religions and training, the dentists in Flagstaff enjoyed an amicable dental family.

Included in my purchase of the practice was a wonderful staff of four women. They accepted me immediately and did everything in their power to make my transition into "their" office seamless. They were very well trained and liked the fact I brought new ideas and techniques to the practice.

Soon another opportunity presented itself, and I ended up taking over the dental office at the Grand Canyon Village (about an hour and a half out of Flagstaff), which at that time had five thousand year-round residents and no dentist.

I took up flying, got my private pilot license and, after a couple of years, tested for and obtained my private pilot instrument rating. I purchased an airplane and flew up to the Grand Canyon once a week to treat my new patients and flew to continuing education classes in Phoenix and California. Flying allowed me to explore the beautiful Southwest part of the country.

Being an avid outdoor enthusiast, I also averaged forty days a year snow skiing. I played competitive racquetball in three states and was a hunter and fisherman.

I had a wonderful life.

Rumors

"I've discovered that the less I say, the more rumors start."

~ *Bobby Clark*

In many ways I was unique to Flagstaff. I say with all due modesty that as a young, unmarried and better-than-average-looking dentist who drove a Corvette and had my own airplane, I held a certain appeal. This uniqueness was enjoyable, but it also came at an odd kind of expense. I kept a quiet but active lifestyle. I certainly wasn't a loud, boisterous braggart, but I *was* the focus of a number of rumors.

One of these suggested that I was a smuggler who used his airplane to cart drugs from Mexico. Outwardly, I laughed off the rumor—it was clear my friends and patients knew it was untrue—but the rumor bothered me and I wondered how it had gotten started. It struck me as one of my mom's favorite sayings coming to pass:

"Michael, good news travels far, but bad news travels farther."

I was fortunate to have a number of Sheriff's deputies and members of the Flagstaff Police Department as patients. Even though they enjoyed ribbing me about the rumor, they also helped trace it back to its source: the wife of one of my dental colleagues who was also a good friend of mine. I was speechless when I found out.

The embarrassment in her eyes when I confronted her with the proof of the police findings was overshadowed by the look of surprise and sadness in the eyes of her unknowing husband. He and I remained friends.

Two years after the rumor, I was approached in a local restaurant by a "friend of a friend" with a business proposition that would supposedly enable me to retire in less than a year.

Who wouldn't listen to that?

All I had to do was make two flights to Ensenada, Mexico, two months apart. Reservations would be made for me at a resort outside of Ensenada for the night, and I would fly back to Arizona the next day. I would be told to ask ground control in Ensenada for a specific tie-down location (private planes are tied down at the wings and tail overnight), and a car would be waiting to take me to a resort. The next morning a car would pick me up, I would fly back to Arizona and land in Tucson, which is a port of entry into the United States from Mexico on the way to Flagstaff. Where I arrived in Tucson, I would again ask for a specific tie-down location. At this point another car would meet me and take me to a resort outside of Tucson for two nights.

This "friend of a friend" didn't mention it, but I knew perfectly well what the cargo would be.

I thanked him for the opportunity but declined his offer. I felt this was a perfect example of the adage, "If it sounds too good to be true, it probably is."

Besides, I had no desire to prove the rumors of my being a drug smuggler true.

The "Kingpin"

A couple of years later I flew my girlfriend as well as my attorney and his wife down to Ensenada to spend a weekend at a resort enjoying the sun and some northern Mexico culture. When we were getting ready to return to Flagstaff, I filed a flight plan and scheduled to clear customs in Nogales, Arizona, which was a port of entry for private flights from Mexico.

Private flying is 95 percent boredom and 5 percent sheer terror. The 95 percent part is flying from point A to point B in beautiful sunny weather; the 5 percent terror is taking off and landing when a crosswind is blowing. That day we were definitely in the 95 percent time and, for the fun of it, I let my attorney take the controls for over half of the flight home. I explained what the different gauges on the instrument panel indicated, and the four of us were having so much fun laughing as we communicated through the microphones in our headsets that we missed an important stop . . .

When I noticed we'd flown past our customs entry at Nogales, I radioed the tower in Tucson, explained my error and was instructed to land in Tucson to clear customs there. After a safe landing, I was instructed by the tower to taxi the plane to a space near a remote hangar, shut the engine down and remain in the plane. We did as we were told.

As soon as the propeller stopped spinning, three vehicles came out of the remote hangar at high speed, two customs agents in each. All of the agents were armed. Three had automatic weapons, and two of them had large German Shepherds on leashes.

Weapons drawn, the agents surrounded the plane.

We were ordered to deplane one at a time, hands above our heads. As soon as we were clear, the two agents with the dogs removed and inspected our luggage. The remaining three agents trained their weapons on us while the commanding officer firmly requested an explanation as to how and why I missed the scheduled customs stop in Nogales.

Apparently, four gringos wearing beach clothing and willing to laugh at their stupidity didn't fit the profile of drug smugglers.

The commander said they'd had our plane on radar for the entire duration of our flight. The smartest thing I'd done, apparently, was to *not* land and take off after the scheduled Nogales clearing was missed. Drug smugglers will typically do precisely this: land, quickly throw out the bales of marijuana they're carrying and take off again, all without shutting down the engines.

Another factor in our favor? The University of Arizona, which is located in Tucson, was playing their in-state rivals Arizona State University in football on television—and the agents were eager to finish the inspection and watch the game. Still, it wasn't until two hours later that us four weary and wayward travelers were allowed to continue on our way to Flagstaff.

For the next six months I bore the nickname "kingpin."

Listen to Your Gut – Lifecoaching Lesson 1

"You have to listen to what resonates within your own gut. You find your direction there."

~ *Kathy Mattea*

I was a perpetual student during my dental career. I enjoyed being up-to-date on new dental techniques, equipment and research and felt my patients deserved the best treatment available. Staying current on the latest developments in my profession was the only way to provide it.

I registered for a continuing education dental course in Park City, Utah, and mentioned my trip to Dan, a business colleague of mine in Flagstaff. When Dan expressed interest in tagging along, I invited him to fly up with me and share the costs of lodging. He and I were avid backcountry skiers and decided to extend our stay for two days, allowing us time to enjoy the "champagne powder" of Utah. We reserved a condo three months in advance, then anxiously waited for the Christmas holiday season and New Year hustle to wind down so we could load the plane and head out.

We left on a beautiful winter day that was brightened by the kind of crisp, blue sky only seen in the mountains. A fresh dusting of glistening white snowcapped the ground and the pine trees surrounding the airport. We taxied down the runway of the Flagstaff airport with our headsets and sunglasses in place and, after a smooth take off, I banked the plane to head in a northwest direction. We were on our way.

I'd chosen a flight path to take us over Canyon Lands National Park, Zion National Park and Arches National Park in southern Utah. The beauty of the ground beneath us was mesmerizing. I had explored these parks from ground level in a four-wheel drive vehicle and remembered admiring the beauty of Mother Nature's artistry, how she shaped the towering rock formations and, with her scalpel, cut steep canyons and carved out beautiful rock arches. Seeing the beauty of the red-hued rocks covered with the fresh white snow from 8,000 feet was breathtaking. Then, rather than staying at 8,000 feet and flying in a straight line, I descended to 3,000 feet and spent some time zig-zagging over the ground below, both Dan and I absorbing the visual bonanza to which we were being treated.

After a smooth landing at a county airport near Park City, we caught a shuttle to our condo. We checked in, then took a walk down the main street. Park City retained, and even enhanced, the charm of an old west ski town—with some concessions. Storefronts were restored to their original colors, but out front they had diagonal parking spots to replace the horse tie-ups. Utah had some very strict liquor laws in those days; all liquor stores were city- or state-owned, and all of the establishments that offered live music entertainment were private clubs. For $5.00 or $10.00 one could become a member of a club, allowing entrance and the ability to buy set-ups (mixers for liquor). Members brought in their own liquor and would pay for the set-ups, uncorking fees for wine, and an opening fee for beer (before tap-top cans). We were both hungry so we found a local lunch spot and, after enjoying an extended lunch hour, decided a nap and shower would feel good before we went out to become "private club members" and find some fun.

Dan and I gladly handed ten dollar bills to the hostess, who handed us our membership cards in return and stamped the backs of our hands as evidence that we were now members. A country music band and a crowded dance floor set the energy level of the club to "fun." No tables were available so we made our way to a bar crowded with couples talking—and singles looking. A man clad in a flight jacket was in front of me and, as he left the bar, opening a spot, he turned and nodded to me.

I felt my stomach tighten and the hair on the back of my neck stand up.

What was that all about? I thought to myself.

But I didn't dwell on it because the bartender was asking me what I needed. Dan and I joined a table with some skiers from Colorado who were also there to experience the champagne powder of Utah. We proceeded to talk, dance, and sing karaoke when the band was on break.

At some point I went to the men's room and ran into the guy with the flight jacket. I had a jacket exactly like it in the condo—I had gotten it in the Army.

I complimented him on his jacket, and this led us to strike up a conversation. Strangely, my stomach tightened *again* but I ignored it, thinking it must be related to being hungry and drinking beer. The guy introduced himself as Jeremy, said he flew helicopters in Viet Nam and said he had moved back to Park City after he got out of the service. I mentioned I had been in the Army the same years as he was in Viet Nam and we shared some guy talk.

My stomach tightened again but I, again, ignored it.

Jeremy told me he had started a scenic helicopter tour company in Park City and asked me if I'd like to take a flight tour of the area first thing in the morning, free of charge. I accepted Jeremy's invitation, told him I'd meet him at the airport at 7:30 a.m., shook his hand and went back to the "table of fun."

***

It seemed like I had only been asleep for fifteen minutes when the alarm buzzed at 6:45 a.m. I got up, turned on the coffee maker and took a quick shower. I pulled on a hooded sweatshirt, some jeans and wool socks and filled my travel mug with freshly-brewed coffee. After putting on my Sorel boots, I took my flight jacket off the coat rack and lifted the hood of my sweatshirt as I put on the jacket. I grabbed a banana, my "Green Airways–Anchorage, Alaska" baseball cap and my sunglasses, and walked down to the corner to grab a shuttle bus to the airport.

Jeremy greeted me outside his hanger. He was dressed like me: jeans, ball cap, sunglasses and flight jacket. He had already pulled the helicopter out of the hangar.

"Morning," he said. "Just finishing up the preflight check."

I admired the helicopter, a Bell 47 with a clear Plexiglass bubble front that would allow excellent sightseeing.

"I'm looking forward to this," I said, even though for some reason I felt my stomach tighten again. This bothered me, and I looked around for some reason as to why it might be happening, but I saw nothing. I figured it must be the coffee and banana—not the perfect breakfast after a hangover.

"It's beautiful country," he said.

The seats were side-by-side; Jeremy climbed in first and I followed. Jeremy reached across me and latched the door, locking it, and he told me how to buckle into the restraint harness. He handed me a pair of headphones that would allow us to communicate while muffling some of the roar of the engine and rotors. Then he checked his instruments one more time, shouted "Clear!" out of his opened window, closed and latched the window and started the rotors.

We lifted straight up ten to fifteen feet and Jeremy pushed the control stick forward.

We were off.

I was amazed at how well the noise-canceling feature of the headphones worked; when I mentioned this to Jeremy he didn't respond, so I assumed he was following the general piloting guidelines of "Aviate-Navigate-Communicate." That is, fly first, make sure you're going the right way, and only then should you start gabbing.

Apparently it wasn't time to communicate. I didn't take it personally.

We were moving at eighty miles an hour and I had a three-hundred-and-sixty-degree view of the beautiful Wasatch mountain range and the houses of Park City, some with smoke rising straight up from their chimneys. The sparkling white ski runs were dotted with large, diesel-driven snowcats grooming the fresh snow that had fallen the night before. In an hour, skiers would be lining up to get into the gondola or wait their turn to occupy a spot on one of the chairlifts that would take them up the mountain for their first run of the day.

After we had flown around the ski area and town for a bit, Jeremy's voice finally came through the headset. He asked if I'd like to see some areas of planned expansion of the ski hill and I responded by nodding my head. Jeremy pulled the control stick towards himself; we banked left and the chopper climbed quickly, allowing us to clear a mountain ridge directly in front of us. As we cleared the ridge, Jeremy's head snapped to the right and he said two words:

"Viet Cong."

The hair stood on the back of my neck and my heart started racing.

We were looking at a beautiful, snow-covered valley with a grove of pine trees on the far end. Two snowmobiles had just emerged from the trees and were cutting through the powder as they headed for another clump of pine trees at the opposite end of the valley.

Jeremy pushed the stick forward. We dropped down the side of the ridge until we were about fifteen feet above the valley floor.

Then he pulled the stick back to level us off and headed directly at the snowmobilers, making the sound of a machine gun with his mouth.

Jeremy's eyes were riveted on the "targets" and an ugly scowl spread across his face.

Imagine being on a snowmobile and a helicopter you don't see, going close to a hundred miles an hour, suddenly buzzes over you only ten feet above. It must have scared the hell out of them.

I know it scared the hell out of *me*. My heart was racing and the adrenaline was pumping through my body, triggering my fight or flight reaction.

After the chopper passed the snowmobilers, Jeremy said, "Missed 'em. We have to take another pass." He banked hard right twice and suddenly we were right behind them again. The awful machine gun fire erupted from Jeremy's mouth once more. Now my anger was directed at Jeremy.

Thankfully there was no time for a third pass; after our second round buzzing them, the snowmobilers had made the safety of the pine trees and stopped. Jeremy banked hard to the left to keep the pine trees between the snowmobilers and the helicopter and we headed back to the airport. He glanced at me and saw the anger in my eyes and the scowl on my face.

It was over before I knew it. Jeremy landed and hurried to open his hangar door. We pulled the tow cart to the chopper, hooked its two arms to the front wheel and easily towed the machine in.

Jeremy closed the door to the hangar, got in his pickup truck and left the airport without saying a word. He wanted nothing to do with me and the anger I exuded. My dad's words rang in my head: "Never start a fight, but never back down, and always get in the first two or three punches." I actually hoped Jeremy would start something.

I stood there, shaken and angry. It was another ten minutes before I could pull myself together and calm down.

Back in Park City, I walked to a coffee shop to grab a coffee and scone. The young girl serving me stared as I pulled my wallet from my front pocket and tried to get a five-dollar bill out of it; my hands were trembling terribly. I hadn't noticed this on the shuttle back to Park City or during the short walk to the coffee shop, but I knew my heart was still beating hard.

I forced a smile and said, "Too much caffeine," then picked up my coffee and scone and sat down in an overstuffed chair by the window. I picked up a day-old local newspaper and there on the back page was an ad for Jeremy's scenic flights.

An older man was sitting in a chair adjacent to mine, and something made me point to the ad and ask him:

"Have you ever taken the scenic flight with Jeremy?"

He took it in stride that a stranger would ask him this out of the blue.

"No. But I'll tell you, my son went into the service the same as Jeremy, though he never actually went to Viet Nam. Jeremy did." And then he added something that made a lot of sense: "It's too bad. Jeremy has never been the same since he got home from Viet Nam."

How right you are, I thought.

***

The experience with Jeremy confirmed a very valuable lesson. There had been a number of situations in my life, prior to Jeremy, when I ignored abnormal internal feelings. In every one of them, I ended up regretting the decision I made. I didn't listen to my intuition telling me to beware.

It's hard for humans to always make the right decisions because sometimes our "egos" (to be explained in greater detail in Part II) are stronger than our common sense. But while we can't always expect to make the right decision, limiting our *wrong* decisions makes our lives much more enjoyable. Intuition can help with this.

Many times simply asking yourself, "Do I want it?" or "Do I need it?" is enough to help find the answers needed to make the correct decision. On the other hand, in many situations, "wanting" is the ego's tool. There are times when it's difficult to get a "read" on one's feelings, and there are times when the luxury to ask the question is not available. For example, if a person is unemployed, asking the "want or need" question might not be in their best interest if they are offered a job—they might simply need to take it. But asking yourself the same question if you're already employed and being offered another job, or another position at the same company, might help your decision.

Helping individuals make decisions by learning to "listen to their gut" was a very enjoyable part of my life-coaching career (which I'll talk about later). Decision making offers us a chance to get in touch with ourselves, to "listen to our gut," to explore what we want in life, and to better understand who we are.

Fortunately, and many years later, I met two remarkable acquaintances who now make it far easier for me to listen to my gut. Their presence in my life has brought a deeper sense of connection to myself and has helped me in all sorts of ways. Oddly enough, they were around even when I took that raucous flight with Jeremy. I just hadn't learned to listen to them yet.

But more on that later.

Almost Losing to Abalone

"Never waste an opportunity to tell someone you love them."

~ *H. Jackson Brown, Jr.*

It was Mother's Day weekend and I was lying on my back, looking up at puffy, white clouds against a beautiful azure sky and imagining their shifting shapes to be animals, people or machines. I felt like I was ten years old again. The main difference was that the wooden floor of the boat was a lot more uncomfortable than the luxurious green grass of my lawn at home.

Only twenty minutes remained of the mandatory hour between my previous dive and the final one of the day. The ocean off the coast of California was calm and the seagulls frolicked above and alongside the dive boat, picking up scraps of food thrown overboard and floating in the wake of the boat. We'd motored slowly from the last dive location; our final site was a large kelp bed. Our target: the elusive abalone shrimp.

I'd received my scuba diver certification and pilot's license the same summer; clearly something in me wanted to explore both the heights and the depths. But for one reason or another I hadn't been on many dive trips. What's more, I hadn't ever dived for abalone, or in kelp.

The dive master explained the dangers of diving in kelp and stressed the importance of staying close to your dive buddy. Scuba divers routinely dive in pairs for safety. In fact, one of the many tests required for certification involves successfully sharing oxygen between two divers—simulating a situation where one diver has malfunctioning equipment. My dive buddy Dan and I had taken and successfully passed the diving certification together and traveled to California for a dive trip. Now we were both excited about reaping the benefits of this final dive: eating the abalone we planned to pluck from the bottom. We felt very comfortable in the water and were excited to spend the day on—and in—the ocean.

The water off the coast of California was cold enough to demand a wet suit for protection from hypothermia. The remainder of my dive gear was made up of a thin rubber dive hood, rubber gloves, a mask with a snorkel attached, two oxygen tanks (with a pressure gauge telling me how much oxygen was available), the breathing regulator, which would be in my mouth, a weight belt, dive knife in a rubber sheath and, of course, full foot fins. We had brought our own masks, fins and knives, and rented the wet suits, weight belts and oxygen tanks. The oxygen in the tanks we wore would last approximately one hour, depending on our rate of breathing.

The dive master explained that the kelp leaves seen on or just below the surface were no reason for concern. Kelp are the trees of underwater forests. Their leaves are connected to flimsy branches, which are in turn connected to the trunks that rise up from the bottom. The branches rhythmically sway with the underwater current, and the real danger lies in the possibility of getting wrapped up in these, which grow quite thick in some areas.

We anchored the boat about a hundred yards from the kelp leaves to avoid getting the propeller shafts tangled in them. Prior to Dan and I entering the water, the dive master threw out a floating buoy with a red flag with a diagonal white line on it; this informed surrounding boats that there were divers in the water.

Dan and I held our masks tight to our faces as we jumped off the boat feet first.

The wetsuit helped, but the first contact with the chilly water still sent a shiver through me—it was a great wakeup call. We exchanged glances and pointed down to start our descent. The kelp branches and trunks were larger and more numerous than expected. They required us to zig-zag left and right as we descended, even as we swam in the general direction of where the abalone were. The deeper we got, the thicker the trunks became.

While concentrating on the zigging and zagging, I committed a cardinal sin of diving: after about fifteen or twenty minutes I lost visual contact with Dan.

Unfortunately, he had made the same mistake. Now I couldn't see him anywhere. The trunks and branches of kelp kept getting thicker and thicker as I swam.

Panic set in and I was aware of my breathing becoming more rapid. This may only be a minor concern above water, but when diving it can cause an obvious problem: the more rapidly you breathe, the more quickly you use up your oxygen. I checked my pressure gauge and I saw I had less than 50 percent of oxygen remaining in my tank.

I decided to ascend and get my bearings.

As I rose I checked the gauge: the 50 percent was now 40 percent. I was breathing harder, using more oxygen, but because of the waving branches and leaves I couldn't go straight up. I still had to zig and zag through the underwater forest and hope I could find a clearer path to the top.

Now, the pressure gauge read 30 percent and I estimated I still had forty or fifty feet to go to get to the safety of the surface.

Branches and leaves brushed against me as I ascended. The more I pushed them aside, the thicker they seemed to get. Twenty percent now, with twenty feet to the top. Breathing rapidly. I became more focused as I knew my air supply was dropping quickly.

Why was my ascent taking so long?

What I didn't realize then was that the branches were clinging to my air tanks, slowing my ascent. I could see the white clouds and blue sky through the water, but it was like looking at them through sunglasses with Vaseline on the lenses. As I pushed the branches and leaves away I realized I was spinning like a slow top—causing the branches to wrap around my legs and arms. I was mummifying myself up in kelp.

Five percent oxygen remaining, with five feet to the surface.

Breathing ever faster.

Now my arms were held tight against my body by thick strands of kelp and I couldn't get to my knife to cut my way out.

Zero percent remaining and my head was bobbing in and out of the water.

Try as I might I couldn't get my hands free to put the snorkel in my mouth. Then I noticed that the breathing end of the snorkel had broken off during my flailing; it wouldn't have mattered even if I *could* have gotten it in my mouth.

Then I had a moment of calm and two thoughts came to mind.

The first: *What a Mother's Day present this is going to be.*

The second, thankfully more useful: *The tanks are held in*

place by straps with two buckles that I can actually reach.

I contorted my wrists to my chest and popped the two buckles open.

Free of the tangled tanks, I floated to the surface. The kelp-ensnared tanks sunk to the bottom. I swam to a nearby rock and pulled myself out of the water, gasping in lungfuls of sweet ocean air.

After a moment I spotted the boat and started waving my arms until they saw me.

It turned out that instead of going directly towards shore, and towards the abalone beds, during all that zigging and zagging through the kelp forest I had inadvertently turned around ninety degrees and been swimming parallel to the shore, going directly *away* from the boat.

Dan wore a worried smile as I climbed the ladder onto the boat. Other divers onboard jumped into the ocean to retrieve my submerged but still-visible tanks.

***

What was learned from this first near-death experience?

Naturally, I learned a lot from it, but the one thing I remembered the most when I couldn't get my hands free to reach my snorkel was thinking: **"There are so many people I didn't get**

a chance to tell how much they meant to me."

To this day I don't hesitate to tell friends and relatives how much they or their friendship means to me. I no longer panic, but instead try to remain calm under extreme pressure. And I realize I am here on earth for a reason.

The search for that reason(s) goes on.

What's more, I believe the same is true for you, too, whether or not you've had your own experience drive that message home for you. Part of the reason I wrote this book was to offer my own experiences in the hopes that they would stimulate your thinking about these issues, and help you explore your own life in a new way. That's what writing this is doing for me.

The Trifecta Before the Big One

The score was 14–12 in my favor and I was serving for game and match point in the semi-final game in the Las Vegas Open Racquetball Tournament. Racquetball was my favorite aerobic sport and I was good at it. I started playing in dental school and became known for my tenacity and quickness, and for my ability to get to almost every opponent's shot. I played competitively in the Army and twice represented Ft. Sill in the 5th Army Racquetball Tournament held in Houston, Texas.

Statistics show dentists have the highest suicide, divorce and alcoholism rates of all medical professionals, and many experts consider stress to be one of the factors for this dubious distinction. I used racquetball as my release from the daily stresses of my dental practice. I played four to five times a week at the Flagstaff Athletic Club, and I enjoyed entering tournaments in Nevada, Utah, Arizona and Southern California.

One more good serve and I was on to the finals against the top player from Las Vegas. I drove a hard, low serve to the right side, my opponent was there and returned a hard shot cross-court. I pushed off on my right foot . . . and heard a loud "POP" that sounded like someone had fired a pistol off next to my ear.

I also experienced the weird sensation of being unable to put my right heel down. Evidently, this is common to a specific injury.

```
DIAGNOSIS: RUPTURED RIGHT ACHILLES
           TENDON.
TREATMENT: SURGERY NEEDED TO RECONNECT
           TORN TENDON; A CAST FROM KNEE
           TO TOES WILL BE NEEDED FOR
           SIX MONTHS; PHYSICAL THERAPY
           TO START TWO WEEKS AFTER
           SURGERY
```

***

Nine months later.

Six to eight inches of fresh snow had fallen overnight at the Snow Bowl Ski Resort, the ski area outside of Flagstaff. I had renewed my season pass, my right leg felt great and I looked forward to the first day on fresh snow. It was to be the first of my average of forty days a year skiing. The cast had been removed the week prior, and the day it was removed I tried my ski boots on. I know a large smile spread across my face as I thought to myself, "Fits like a glove. I can't wait."

My best ski buddy, Boz, and I lowered the tips of our skis to the snow and slid off the chair of the Agassiz Chairlift at the top of the Inner Basin Run. We both buckled the top buckle of each boot and skied down about a hundred yards to get the blood flowing to our legs. We pulled our goggles away from our faces to defog them and smiled at each other. Boz reached around and snapped the goggle strap on the back of my helmet. He shouted something—most likely a slight obscenity—as he started skiing again, making three beautiful slalom turns on the steep part of the run.

I always admired Boz's skiing form: nothing moved but his shins, calves and ski boots, and his knees absorbed all the compression. When Boz wasn't present, I described his form to others as "poetry in motion." Even though Boz was twelve years younger than me, we had become good friends shortly after he came into my dental office as a new patient. We shared the outdoor interests of snow skiing, water skiing, wind surfing and golfing, but most of all we enjoyed each other's company and sense of humor. Neither one of us missed a chance to "punk" the other one.

Three turns of my own and I was following Boz down the freshly groomed run. Halfway down to the chair lift, the Inner Basin Run merged with a beginners' Green run. As we neared the merging area, both Boz and I slowed down to avoid any chance of a collision with beginner skiers. We skied next to each other briefly, then Boz made a sharp turn to the right which showered my face with snow. I reached up to brush the snow off my goggles and, when I looked up, realized I was on a collision course with a little girl snow-plowing down the hill.

I stood hard on my right ski and made a sharp turn to the left to avoid colliding with the little girl. Unfortunately, the left side of the run was lined with dense, mature trees. I avoided the first tree but my left shoulder slammed into the tree directly behind it and I fell to the ground. Intense, stabbing pain rose up and I immediately started sweating profusely. The pain in my shoulder increased as I struggled to stand up. I needed to stand to be able to step into the binding of the right ski that had released, but the snow was deep and it covered the binding. I fell over again, unable to maintain my balance in the deep snow. Unfortunately, I landed directly on my left shoulder. The snow was deeper than I thought. I was sweating from the effort to get up. Finally I was able to clear away the snow, I stepped into my binding, sidestepped my way out onto the ski run and slowly started skiing down to the lodge. The only way I could get some relief from the pain was to hold my left arm at a ninety-degree angle.

Boz didn't realize I had challenged a tree and lost. He'd skied down to the lift and was waiting for me in line to go back up the mountain. He looked up at me as I skied past the lift towards the lodge carrying two poles in my right hand, doing my best Napoleon impersonation with my left hand tucked into my ski jacket. He couldn't see the pain in my eyes and he got on the next chair as a single.

Two members of the ski patrol were waiting for me as I skied into the area outside the patrol entry. They immediately knew the shoulder was dislocated and that resetting it as soon as possible would be in my best interest. One patrolman took my poles and removed my goggles and helmet while the other helped me get up on a table. They had me lay face down on the table with my left arm hanging over the side, totally unsupported. They knew the pain I was feeling and distracted me with conversation while one of them went under the table, gripped my arm and pulled it down and forward. The pain was excruciating, but it was immediately replaced by relief the moment my shoulder clicked back into its socket. The ski patrolmen fashioned a rudimentary sling out of a towel and I waited about fifteen minutes in the ski patrol shack for Boz to come and find me. We knew the patrolmen well and had spent time swapping lies with them in the past.

Boz came in and said, "You're going to keep that towel, aren't you? The second run was better than the first, and you missed it." It was the sarcastic sense of humor that we shared and he knew I would probably say the same thing if our roles were reversed. I just shook my head and anxiously looked forward to getting home to take pain medication and muscle relaxants.

> DIAGNOSIS: SEVERLY DISLOCATED SHOULDER
>   WITH TORN ROTATOR CUFF AND
>   SURROUNDING LIGAMENTS.
> TREATMENT: SHOULDER SURGERY FOLLOWED BY
>   SIX MONTHS OF PHYSICAL
>   THERAPY.

***

Six months later.

The shoulder felt strong after I completed the rigorous physical therapy program and I was anxious to get back on the racquetball court. I had frequented the club to work out over the six months of rehab and watched with envy the racquetball players with their steamed goggles and sweat-soaked t-shirts. I had heard a couple of good, new players had moved into Flagstaff and, as I was the defending club champion, I knew I'd have a target on my back.

People often want to take down the king of the hill . . . and in this case, that king was me.

The day arrived: I got the release from my surgeon to return to athletics. A wide smile graced my face as I walked in the front door of the Flagstaff Athletic Club. The receptionist came out from behind the counter to welcome me back and give me a big hug. I kissed her on the forehead and thanked her for the nice thoughts. I acknowledged other "welcome backs" and headed directly for the locker room to change into my slightly used racquetball shoes, clean gym shorts and t-shirt. I opened the package containing a new racquetball glove, tossed the wrapper in the trash and slid my hand into the soft leather glove. I reached up and, from the top shelf of my locker brought down an eyeglasses case, opened it and took out a pair of clear eye-protector goggles. I stretched the strap over my head and pulled the goggles down over my eyes to see if the strap needed adjusting. No adjustment needed. I grabbed my towel, turned the combination on the lock after I closed my locker and left for Court #3.

I introduced myself to the twenty-something "kid" named Joe who was my opponent. I explained I was coming off of a long layoff and I didn't know how long my aerobic capacity would allow me to play, but that I looked forward to working up a good sweat. Joe nodded, said he understood and that he would take it easy on me. Even though the words were said with sincerity, I felt the adrenaline start pumping at the challenge. We lobbed for serve and I won. I was serving 0-0.

My first serve was a lob serve to Joe's backhand. Joe responded with a cross court shot to my forehand side. As I pushed off on my left foot I again heard the sickening sound of a loud

"POP," but this time it was accompanied by an intense, sharp pain running up my left calf.

```
DIAGNOSIS: RUPTURED LEFT ACHILLES
           TENDON.
TREATMENT: SURGERY TO RECONNECT TENDON;
           TO BE FOLLOWED BY SIX MONTHS
           OF REHAB AND PHYSICAL
           THERAPY.
```

And, I didn't even get to work up a good sweat.

***

What the hell was going on?

The effects of stress are cumulative in an individual, and, when the effects become dangerous, they'll take the path of least resistance out of the body. Racquetball was my stress release tool and I was now going on three years without a stress release vehicle. Unbeknownst to me, my body and the universe were trying to tell me to slow down.

Unfortunately, I wasn't listening.

The Big One

I'm sitting on the balcony of my hotel overlooking Mission Bay in San Diego, drinking a glass of fresh squeezed orange juice and watching three seagulls dip and dive in their quest for the next eatable treat. The ocean bay is fairly calm, with very small waves settling onto the well-groomed beach. The resort is gradually waking up, providing its guests with everything we desire.

I have to admit that after three surgeries and three rehabilitations, as well as being present in support of a sister going through divorce, this vacation to do some catamaran sailing and windsurfing is much needed. I've been in vacation mode for three days and I've slept like a baby each night. In fact, for the first time in years I've slept in past eight o'clock in the morning. There seems to be a sense of relaxation mixed with energy in the people I've run into, and I'm sure I exude the same to them.

The day before I had taken a catamaran sailing lesson and by noon felt proficient enough to take a Hobie Cat out by myself and cruise the entire bay area. I even ventured out a little way into the Pacific Ocean. I had done a lot of windsurfing and found that handling the wind while sailing a catamaran was exactly the same. While sailing I saw some individuals on windsurfers taking advantage of the steady ocean breezes and knew I was going to be one of them this afternoon. I had scheduled an ocean-racing windsurfer lesson from one of the local shops on the bay and was to meet my instructor, Brian, at noon at the shop to sign all of the insurance forms, waivers, and so on. The forecast was for the wind to increase to a comfortable level about noon. I was excited to windsurf in a steady breeze as opposed to windsurfing near Flagstaff, where instead of steady breezes we were accustomed to gusty winds that could quickly change direction and launch a person off their board. So I looked forward to the lesson, after which I was meeting Dave—a good friend of mine from Flagstaff who was going to law school in San Diego—for dinner.

***

The paperwork is complete. Brian explains the strategy of racing and sets me up with a racing windsurfer board and sail—the board is shorter and the sail smaller than the equipment I've used in the past, and they are a lot more responsive. Out on the water we sit on our boards and talk; Brian reminds me of the techniques and strategy we discussed earlier.

Then we stand up, hook our harnesses onto the mast, position our sails to grab the greatest amount of wind and . . . *fly* across the water. The speed and responsiveness of the boards is exhilarating, and I'm sure everyone within a five-mile radius can see my smile and hear me yell, "Oh, yeah! That's what I'm talkin' about!"

As soon as I yell I feel my harness release and find myself flying through the air.

I splash in a heap, laughing, and climb back on the board, stand up—and immediately fall off again.

I get back on the board, feeling dizzy.

What's happening?

Why does the ocean water look a different shade of blue than it did when I started my lesson?

I'm looking straight ahead . . . and I'm seeing double . . . Everything is shaking side-to-side. I hear Brian yelling, but I can't make out his words.

What is happening?

I've never had a headache before, but now it feels like someone is pounding on the back of my head with a hammer. I lie down on my board and wrap my arms around it so I won't fall off. Brian paddles over to me and I hear him asking what's wrong . . . *but I can't lift my head to answer him.*

Brian waves his arms and I hear the sound of an outboard

motor drawing close and stopping. I feel myself being lifted into the boat—but why can't I use my right arm to help them?

I'm feeling nauseous and getting sick to my stomach.

Brian and the boat driver take me to shore and call 911. Soon I hear the voice of an ambulance driver telling me I'll be okay. He asks my name and I struggle against the beating on the back of my head and the dry heaves rising from my stomach to answer . . . But I fail, and the driver must see the fear in my eyes, because he doesn't ask me again.

***

The next thing I remember is waking up on a small bed with a blood pressure cuff on my left arm. My bed is encircled by a privacy curtain. A friendly female nurse's face looks down at me and says,

"Hi, Doctor. You're in the emergency room and your doctor will be here shortly. Don't try to talk." She hands me a pen. "Please sign this consent to treatment form."

Through my double vision I take the pen as she holds up the clipboard with the form and points to the line next to a yellow "X."

I lower the pen towards the form . . . but I can't get anywhere near the piece of paper, much less the yellow "X." I feel a frightening disconnection from my body and fear surges through me.

She gently guides my hand to the clipboard and softly says, "Just make an X, if you can. You're doing fine"

I do my best, all the while thinking to myself, "Can't they do something about that damn hammer beating on the back of my head?"

***

"Hello, I'm Dr. Simons. I'm a neurologist." I look up and see a tall, thin man, approximately my age, with a receding hairline, looking down at me. A slight, but encouraging, smile lies beneath his thin mustache. The pain in the back of my head has become a dull ache now. "Could you please put both arms straight out to your sides then touch the tip of your nose with the forefinger of each hand?"

This sounds like a simple enough request, I think to myself.

With my left hand I can easily touch my nose . . . but when I try with my right hand I can't even hit my *head* with my finger.

The same fear I'd experienced in the ambulance grips me all over again. What is *wrong* with me? Why is my body failing me? And the back of my head is throbbing again.

He says, "I'm going to order a spinal tap ASAP to see if there's any blood in your spinal fluid."

Spinal tap? That sounds painful. And why my spine? My mind is now swimming all over with the worst case scenarios of not ever being able to use my right arm again or, even worse, of being paralyzed for the rest of my life.

A young, right-handed dentist with no right side! Now I'm real scared, and I'm sure the fear shows in my eyes, because they're filled with tears.

DIAGNOSIS: LEFT BRAINSTEM STROKE CAUSED
BY THE PINCHING OFF OF THE
LEFT VERTEBRAL ARTERY.
PROGNOSIS: USUALLY FATAL OR RESULTING IN
COMA.

Hurdles Follow a Huge Mistake

"Experience is simply the name we give our mistakes."

~ *Oscar Wilde*

At the time of my stroke I was, by normal standards, a success. I was young, in excellent condition, and I didn't lead a stressful life. I had a good income and a number of assets: a beautiful home, two cars, and a successful dental practice—not to mention a plane to fly back and forth between them.

But as competent of a dentist as I was, I made a critical mistake at the beginning of my dental career. At the time I didn't realize my *biggest* asset was my ability to produce a good income, so unfortunately I didn't consider purchasing disability insurance.

Consequently, a career-ending accident at age thirty-six reduced me, within a relatively short span of time, to living on a hundred dollars a week.

Disability insurance is designed to cover a person's income potential. I was the last person anyone thought would need disability insurance. I was in excellent shape and led an active, healthy life. (And in fact, being young and in good condition were the two things that did actually save my life.) What's more, without a dental practice I could not accrue the income I'd planned on to someday retire comfortably. After the accident, all of the money I'd saved and invested in my retirement plan was needed for daily living.

The savings and investment income only lasted so long.

My stroke hit me out of nowhere. It affected me profoundly, throwing my "perfect" life for a loop and leaving me emotionally devastated and at loose ends. I will talk more about that later, but regardless of this aspect of things, the practical repercussions of the stroke were also front and center, and they had to be dealt with.

Physically, it affected my right side. I couldn't walk up steps, and going up a ramp was very difficult. Effectively, the stroke ended my career as a dentist by taking away the fine motor skills in my right hand. It also affected my internal clock significantly by completely reversing my wake and sleep times. I was awake most of the night and slept most of the day. But fatigue limited my waking periods to three or four hours at a time. I learned that the times of sleep were of utmost importance, as those were when my body was doing the majority of its healing. A prescription for a sleeping aid from my doctor enabled me to finally get some good, consecutive nights of restful sleep. When I ran out of the prescription there was one refill available and I filled it immediately. When the refill ran out I called my doc and asked him to write another prescription for the medication but he refused my request, saying the drug was extremely addictive and he didn't want me to get hooked on it.

Hell—I was already hooked! Had I become dependent on a drug in three weeks? The fragile state of my psyche compounded my dependency on the drug. I had trouble sleeping for longer than four hours at a time. When I mentioned this to the doctor he wrote me a prescription for another medication that wasn't addictive but which helped me to sleep soundly and, more importantly, continue the healing process.

The whole experience, brief as it was, gave me a tremendous amount of empathy and understanding for individuals who become dependent on medications for pain relief, insomnia, and so on. In my case, my lack of sleep made it remarkably easy to come close to getting addicted to my insomnia medication. Sleep is such a fundamental need that you can't go long without it, and the discomfort when you try to do so is enough to make one risk desperate measures.

Another side effect of my stroke was that I had no control over my emotions. If something was funny, I would laugh hard enough to be unable to speak and tears would flow as if turned on by a faucet. And if something were the least bit sad (for example, a television commercial showing abused children or dogs), I would tear up easily, with that same faucet turned all the way on. Many of the other emotions I experienced are recorded in my book *A Stroke Patient's Own Story – A Personal Guide for Rehabilitation.*[2]

I was very fortunate to have six different dentists take over my practice and treat my patients for the six months immediately following the stroke. Keeping the office open, patients treated and my staff in place ultimately allowed me to sell my practice. Even so, in the end, I sold it at a discounted price to make sure my patients would be well taken care of. (I had sold the Grand Canyon practice two years before the stroke.)

My landlord thankfully told me not to worry about the rent while I was out of the office those six months. Because I was able to sell most of my assets, I significantly reduced the debt I carried.

As for my remaining debtors, I contacted each of them, explained the situation and arranged repayment plans. I was determined to pay back every dollar I owed. And for two and a half years I made every one of my negotiated payments on time, even though I wasn't getting ahead financially. I was content to concentrate on my speech, occupational and physical therapies.

---

[2] Personal note: if you or someone you know is a stroke survivor and would like an email copy of this book, contact me at bookernmike@gmail.com and it would be my pleasure to send it to you.

Then another hurdle presented itself. Out of the blue, my landlord suddenly decided to escalate the repayment of the back rent due and demanded payment of $18,000, to be paid back immediately. I have no idea why he decided to do this.

Of course, the post-hospitalization directives I received from my doctors included keeping stress to a minimum. My body had gone through tremendous stress after the stroke and it would be healing itself for a number of years. The abrupt and unexpected escalation of the debt repayment threw me into a tailspin of sleeplessness that demanded a short stay in the hospital. Upon the advice of my accountant and attorney I filed for bankruptcy protection.

In fact, shortly after the stroke my advisors had suggested the very same thing, but I was raised to pay my debts—no matter the costs.

I never told my parents or sisters about my hospital stay or subsequent bankruptcy. I could have blamed the situation on how I was raised—after all, my life would have been a lot easier if I hadn't decided I had to pay back all my debts. But in reality, how I was raised had nothing to do with it. I know now that a stroke is a brain injury that not only affects physical abilities but also one's thought processes and judgment. What this meant was that the strong work ethic and personal pride that were such indelible parts of my makeup actually worked against me. I could have used an additional dose of humility, even though I had just received a huge one in the form of the stroke. But instead I was too proud to listen. Had I been thinking clearly or consulted a trusted friend, I believe I would've taken my advisors' sound advice and filed for bankruptcy earlier. This would've let me devote my energies to my therapy without being distracted by the burden of debt hanging over me. I think this would have allowed me to heal faster.

But as they say, hindsight is 20/20.

It took me five years to fully relearn to walk, talk and write, and I now carry a credit score of 807. So, it worked out, but I could have made those five years a lot easier by being easier on my psyche and more understanding with myself.

A Great Result from a Questionable Decision

In one way my refusal to ask for help worked in my favor, though it didn't seem that way at first. After my stroke, I asked my parents not to come to Flagstaff to help me. I really don't know why I requested this, though I do know it hurt their feelings. As you can imagine, most parents would want to be there for their children in such a time. It would have been very reasonable for them to have moved in with me and helped with all the normal daily activities that had to get done. But I refused this help.

Why?

I couldn't have told you at the time. It wasn't until years later that I realized the reason for my request. Now I think that part of the answer was that the Universe was looking out for me.

Years after the stroke I sat my parents down around the same kitchen table that had provided us with so many good, loving memories, and I said something I'd never forget saying.

"Mom and Dad, thank you for honoring my wishes not to come

to Flagstaff after my stroke. At the time I didn't know why I asked that of you, but today I know. I can't imagine how hard it was for you to respect my wishes and not be present in the time of need of your firstborn child. To be honest, I don't know if I could have done it if I'd had kids of my own.

"But if you'd come, I know you'd have done every little thing I needed. And I would've let you do them. But as it turned out, the way it was, there was no one there to do those things. I had to do everything, and I now realize that all those hours of doing simple, daily-living chores were actually extra therapy for me. I wouldn't be standing here today having people say things like 'You'd never know you had a severe stroke' if I hadn't had those extra hours of therapy."

When I'd finished talking, I saw the love in their eyes, and I knew they understood.

Thankfully, I had figured this out and explained it to them when they were both cognizant and understanding. As a result, our relationship grew even deeper after my explanation.

Going Forward

"You are always a student, never a master.
You have to keep moving forward."

~ *Conrad Hall*

After selling my practice I moved to the Phoenix area. My thinking was that whatever I ended up doing for the rest of my life would probably have to take place in a metropolitan area. Flagstaff was a small town and since I was no longer able to be a dentist, a larger city would offer more opportunities and choices for future careers than Flagstaff could.

From the get-go I tried to be productive: I founded the International Stroke Foundation, formed a respectable board of directors and enlisted the help of a state Senator to help expedite the Foundation's 501(c)(3) non-profit status application. I wrote the book for stroke survivors in which I explained what I did for rehabilitation after exhausting the conventional therapies provided me. Later, with the generous help of the Merck Company

Foundation, I oversaw the production of a video that aired on PBS entitled, "Stroke: So Common, So Ignored."

Knowing that the book and the television program touched thousands of lives and, hopefully, helped prevent a stroke somewhere, was very rewarding to me. However, running a non-profit organization that depended on individual donations didn't provide me with an income sufficient to move me above the poverty line.

I had to find a job. Since I could no longer practice dentistry, I sought out the services of a clinical psychologist to help me figure out possibilities for what I could do with the rest of my life. The provider I found put me through a battery of tests, the results of which were compared to those of individuals in varying professions.

Practically speaking, the results showed I was definitely a people person. They also indicated I was an excellent listener, had high integrity, and that people trusted and believed me; in short, I would be excellent in sales. Interestingly, because I participated in many sports and am an avid sports spectator, "sportscaster" was also high on the list. That profession was ruled out since I was still working with a speech therapist to regain my speech. I had to admit that a sportscaster who couldn't talk very well and who slurred his speech would be rather comical.

One of the tests involved having me prepare a list of the ten best things and the ten worst things that had happened to me in my life. I was instructed to take two weeks to compile these lists.

At the end of those two weeks I found something very surprising about my answers: I had listed "stroke" on both lists. In other words, I felt my stroke was one of the best *and* worst things that had happened to me.

How could this be?

I could easily understand listing the stroke as one of the worst things to happen to me because it had taken my livelihood and identity away from me. It had turned my physical world upside down. Materially speaking, before the stroke I had everything I desired.

Shortly after the diagnosis I learned that the type of stroke I had usually results in death or leaves the survivor comatose. So, while I did list it as one of the worst things to happen to me in my life, I could begin to accept that I was also fortunate in a way, and that something else was at work in my life. I believe the list was the catalyst for me to find the reason my life was spared. I look at surviving the stroke as being the beginning of my search for internal, not external, happiness.

There were also some strange and humorous after-effects of the stroke. While in high school and junior college I was active in musical operetta productions and two of my high school classmates and I formed a musical trio. The name we chose was a mixture of our last names—the Prazlinton Trio. We performed at senior resident homes and on stage for our high school talent competitions. We never won anything but we had fun and sounded pretty good (I must admit). For a long time after my stroke I was unable to carry a tune when I tried to sing.

Even stranger, I couldn't whistle—either using my fingers or simply blowing. Evidently, the rehabilitation to regain my speech did not affect the part of the brain that controls the muscles in the tongue and cheek that would allow me to whistle. To this day I can't whistle at all but I'm a bit better at carrying a tune.

In any case, I know I'm here for another reason, and, personally, I believe everything happens for a reason. My stroke helped me realize that.

All Dressed Up But Nowhere to Go

Job 1 A.D.

(After **D**entistry)

I couldn't practice dentistry any longer, but the stroke hadn't taken away my ability to use my education and experience. I was still willing and able to read x-rays, review doctors' records and treatment plans, and record my unbiased findings with recommendations as to whether care given in specific cases was adequate or not. So I formed a corporation named MyCorp, Inc. (pretty original, huh?), which was retained by insurance companies and attorneys in defense of dentists in malpractice suits.

Often the cases were fairly clear, but on a number of cases I was asked by attorneys to edit legal reports in their clients' best interest. When I received these requests, my father Nick's words always resonated in my head: "Son, the two most important things you have in life are your *integrity* and your *reputation*. They will follow you everywhere."

I never changed my findings, despite multiple requests and a certain degree of pressure from the people who hired me.

I was once called as an expert witness in a malpractice suit. On this occasion I was asked by the defense attorney to "color" my statement in favor of his client. I refused, and after the court rendered its decision, I was called in to the judge's chambers. I didn't know what to expect and, understandably, I was a bit nervous.

There was no need to be. When I sat down at the judge's desk, he said simply, "Dr. Prazich, thank you for your testimony and for your *integrity*. I was told you were solicited by one of the parties to alter your report and that you wouldn't oblige him. On behalf of the plaintiff, I thank you." I appreciated and was humbled by his praise; after all, all I had done was tell the truth as I saw it.

As I left his office, I remembered again my father's words and said to myself, *Thank you, Dad.*

Unfortunately, as noble as my intentions were, the services I offered through MyCorp, Inc., weren't in as much demand as I had hoped.

I needed to press on to find new sources of income.

A Guy's Gotta Do What He's Gotta Do

Job 2 A.D.

(After Dentistry)

I answered an ad in the newspaper and took a sales job selling earthquake-proof supports for mobile homes. My compensation was based purely on sales commissions, and I had to provide my own coveralls, clipboard and flashlight.

After a one-week training program I began crawling under trailer homes and reporting my findings to the clients who had called for a free housing analysis. I represented a product that could limit or prevent damage to mobile homes in the event of an earthquake. I approached my clients with my findings exactly as I would have had they been new dental patients with whom I was going over x-rays. I always arrived well-groomed and on time, and in two months I became the top salesperson in the three-state region.

I learned two lessons while on this job.

First, I was humbled by my situation. I had gone from being a dentist and flying my own airplane to crawling under trailer houses in coveralls and trying to convince mobile home owners to buy a product I really didn't believe was essential. I sold earthquake supports that were supposed to protect mobile homes from extensive damage in the event of an earthquake. I know Arizona borders California but I'll bet it had been quite a while since an earthquake hit Phoenix, Arizona. An increased sense of *humility* was inescapable and it was joined by a sense of embarrassment. Sometimes, a guy's got to do what he's got to do to survive.

Second, I gained a sense of *compassion* and *respect* for working individuals whose compensation is based solely on sales commissions. A good salesperson can make an excellent income; sales is a wonderful profession for the individual who doesn't want to be confined to an office all day and who is not lacking in self-confidence. Making a living through sales based on commission was 180 degrees away from making a living as a medical professional where people came to me to make their lives better.

The biggest hurdle to living on commissions is making that first sale. It might take a dozen presentations to make a sale but, once you've got that under your belt, you boost your confidence and get a little money in your pocket to treat yourself. Confidence is the key.

I carried both of these lessons with me into my next job.

**

- **Humility** (adjectival form: **humble**) is variously seen as the act or posture of lowering oneself in relation to others. Humility by definition can also be the quality or condition of being humble.[3]

- **Compassion,** noun: sympathetic pity and concern for the sufferings or misfortunes of others.[4]

---

[3] *Wikipedia.*
[4] *Oxford Living Dictionaries.* Accessed February 15, 2017.
https://en.oxforddictionaries.com/definition/compassion

Better Doin' But Still Just Doin'

Job 3 A.D.

(After Dentistry)

A friend of mine asked if I would be interested in a job paying higher commissions—and which didn't require crawling under trailer homes.

The job involved selling home water purification systems to individuals who responded to a telemarketer asking if they'd like their water tested for free. The Phoenix area has very hard water and contains many minerals. Fortunately, the filtration product I would be selling was a quality appliance, and I firmly believed in its value.

The appointments were made for me. Clients had already been qualified as interested buyers over the telephone. I would arrive— on time and well-groomed—to test their water, give them a well-rehearsed presentation, and show them the cleaning potential of purified water. I inserted a relaxed sense of humor into the presentation and made sure the homeowners got involved. I knew my product well, but more importantly I knew my competitors' products even better. I enjoyed "showing and telling" the benefits of pure water and the advantages of this particular filtration system.

My presentation-to-closing ratio was excellent and, like with Job 2 A.D., I quickly became recognized as one of the top sales producers in the country. I was profiled in the industry magazine and saved enough money to buy a used Audi for $3,000.

I had to buy it with cash because, due to the recent bankruptcy, I couldn't secure acceptable financing—another reminder of humility!

***This time I treated myself with compassion.* I learned later in my life how important self-compassion and self-recognition are to an individual and, without knowing what I had done, I had actually acknowledged my success and praised myself. Somehow I knew the stroke was part of my personal journey, and I had a strong feeling that I was going to be successful again.** Again, I thanked Nick and X for the work ethic they had imparted to me.

Making Sure What Happened to Me Didn't Happen to Someone Else

Job 4 A.D.

(After Dentistry)

After over two years of speech therapy and a lot of work following that, I regained "acceptable speech." I still spoke more slowly, because it was more comfortable for me to do so. I still had to think about the words and the pace of my speech, which was slower than before the stroke. On the other hand, I was now very succinct with my speech, enunciating my words and making sure the person(s) to whom I was speaking could see my lips and my eyes. I always made direct eye contact. These actions weren't intentional at first, but they had excellent results.

I was asked to address the Arizona Medical Association and the Arizona Dental Association regarding the need for doctors and dentists to have good disability insurance in place. What happened to me made me a poster child for what could happen to any successful medical professional without disability insurance coverage in place. I basically told them my story and, when I was done speaking, a couple of gentlemen in attendance asked me if I would consider doing seminars for them. They owned an insurance agency in Arizona and their primary market was the medical professional. The caveat, however, was that the only way I could make a living over and above an hourly wage doing the seminars was to get my insurance license and become an insurance professional.

So that's what I did. Before long I had my insurance license and was hired by the two gentlemen who had offered me the seminar job. I was extremely excited to start a new career. The company sent me to school to learn about the product I would be representing. On my own, I duplicated what I had done when setting out to sell the water purification product: I learned about every other disability insurance product on the market. It made sense to me to know who my competition was and what their products offered. I was getting paid to learn, and my compensation was based on a draw against future commissions—a big change from being compensated 100 percent on the commissions earned from sales.

Because of my history as a dentist, I was fairly well known in the Arizona dental community. I called every dentist I knew (and many I didn't know) to set up a time to talk, and to explain how I wanted to make sure what happened to me didn't happen to them. Of course, my own story spoke for itself.

I took advantage of my history and connections as a dentist. Most insurance agents prefer doctors and dentists as clients because medical professionals have high insurance needs, and this translates into higher commissions for the agents. Because medical professionals are "clients in demand," they are inundated with phone calls from insurance agents wanting to take them to lunch or meet after work. Most of my telephone calls were answered by a receptionist who didn't know me. But when they took my message I had the advantage of being able to say, "Can you please have Dr.____ call Dr. Prazich at his earliest convenience?" Most called back, and if they were well insured I offered congratulations and told them to call me if they needed any advice.

From my perspective, I had a story to tell and it was easy for me to tell it. I was genuinely sincere and never a "high-pressure" salesman. I considered myself a dentist first and foremost; I tried to put my prospects in my shoes and I truthfully told them I'd always be looking out for their best interests.

After my first year in the insurance business I was recognized by one of the largest life and disability insurance companies in the United States as one of their Top 10 Disability Insurance Producers in the country. My production numbers qualified me to be named to the company's Inner Circle of Top Producers Club.

I remained in the insurance business—Job 4 A.D.—for over twenty-two years and was a member of the Inner Circle for over fifteen years. After having to leave dentistry, I feel very blessed to have found a career that stimulated me psychologically and caused me to empathize with the many individuals who have had to redefine their lives and careers due to the loss of their jobs, and through no fault of their own.

Louisa

*"The meeting of two personalities is like the contact of two
chemical substances; if there is any reaction,
both are transformed."*

~ *Carl Jung*

I continued the post-stroke therapy sessions I had started in
Flagstaff even after I took up selling insurance. In most cases,
individuals who are recovering from neurological trauma have
trouble with dexterity and their fine motor skills. My occupational
therapy sessions consisted of doing simple daily tasks over and
over and over, training new brain cells to do what the cells
destroyed by the stroke once did.

For example, the normal process of action in a muscle is for the
energy to go from Point A to Point B to Point C, unimpeded. If the
point B cell is destroyed by a neurological accident (stroke),
rehabilitation trains the brain to go from A to C, but this time
through D, instead of the destroyed B. Simply stated, the brain is
trained to achieve the same results as before, only using different
pathways.

One of the exercises I had to do consisted of taking pennies out of one cup with my right hand and placing them in another cup. This simple task was a challenge for me. I had trouble putting my fingers together to grab the pennies. At such times my frustration was very visible and I would get up from the table and walk away.

"Don't be so hard on yourself, Michael. It only gets better."

The statement came from Louisa, a volunteer occupational therapy assistant, as I was doing an exercise one day. Louisa was ten or fifteen years my senior, and she had a calming voice and demeanor. She had quickly picked up on the fact that I was a competitive person, and she explained how being competitive was a negative for rehabilitation. Something about Louisa made me want to try harder in my rehabilitation and get to know her better as a person.

She said, **"*Perseverance* and *patience* are keys to rehabilitation and in life as well. You can't worry about the things you have no control over."**

A week later I was browsing in a bookstore and noticed the title of a small book, *Don't Sweat the Small Stuff and It's All Small Stuff.*[5] I smiled and thought: *The author must have met Louisa at some point.*

I purchased the book and gave it to Louisa as a gift. She and I gradually became good friends, and she would schedule her volunteer days to coincide with my therapy sessions.

---

[5] Carlson, Richard. *Don't Sweat the Small Stuff . . . and It's All Small Stuff.* New York, NY: Hyperion, 1997.

One day, after we had finished the work, Louisa and I were sitting on a bench outside the office. We each had a cup of Chai Tea and were enjoying the warm, spring day.

Louisa said, "Have you ever heard of 'channeling'?"

I shook my head—no.

Louisa smiled and explained that some individuals are blessed with a gift: they can serve as the mouthpiece for an older being or spirit, in essence becoming a "channel" for them. I asked her if I had to be hypnotized and, with her warm smile and calming voice, she said, "No."

Then she caught me off guard.

"Michael, I'm a channel. Would you like to be channeled?"

I didn't hesitate. I've always been one to try anything once. What's more, I trusted Louisa and was interested in seeing this side of her.

I said, "You bet I would!"

My curiosity was piqued when she first started explaining channeling, but it was intense now—at the thought of experiencing it firsthand.

We agreed on a time to meet. I went home and immediately started seeking out information about "channeling" on the web. The search results varied tremendously, so I shut down my computer and said to myself, "Let's just do this, Michael".

Channeling

"Each department of knowledge passes through three stages; the theoretical stage, the theological stage and the metaphysical or abstract stage."

~ Auguste Comte

I was sitting on Louisa's love seat when she came in with a pot of hot water for tea. I was looking forward to whatever was going to happen; I likened sitting there to standing alone at the top of a ski run with only untracked powder before me.

Louisa poured a cup of tea and said she was a channel for an old Irish spirit named Ian. She explained that she was going to put her head down for a short time and, when her head came up, I shouldn't be frightened or surprised at what I heard. She placed a cassette into the recorder on her coffee table, pressed the "record" button and put her head down.

The recorder hummed as it started, and I waited quietly.

"Hello, I am Ian." The voice came from Louisa, who had raised her head, but it sounded more like a *male* voice than Louisa's usual tone. What's more, it was flavored with a strong Irish brogue.

I was silent at first because I was surprised. Then I introduced myself, and ended up sitting quietly as he spoke for the next half hour.

He knew things about me about which Louisa had no clue. Things I had not, in fact, shared with *anybody*. He knew my best friend was killed in a senseless war (his words) and that I had two sisters, and so on.

At one point Ian explained that every person has at least one "spirit guide" who has been around their entire life and who is always with them. He told me I was very fortunate because I had *two* guides, one male and one female.

"I can't hear the male's name clearly," he said. "It sounds like Joseph, and I know it's a name from the Old Testament." He seemed to have a moment of minor frustration at not being able to catch the name. Then he said, as if giving up trying to find out, "Oh, you'll know. The name of your female guide is Leah."

Ian talked for a while longer until saying, "I have to go now, I'm tired. You'll like your guides, Michael." Then "his" head dropped down, and when it came back up again, there was Louisa.

Her first words were: "Did you meet Ian?"

She hit the "stop" button, opened the door of the recorder and handed me the cassette. She knew nothing of my conversation with Ian, but she looked tired, and I could tell the half hour with Ian took a lot out of her physically. We chatted for a while longer and, as I walked out the door and down Louise's sidewalk, Ian's words rang in my ears.

"Oh, you'll know . . ."

At the time I was a big fan of the Irish band, U2. I started my car and the radio came on. As I pulled out of the driveway the announcer said, "Here's a song from U2's newly-released album, The **Joshua** Tree."

I hit the brakes. Ian's words echoed in my head: "It sounds like Joseph . . . It's a name from the Old Testament."

I knew right away that the name of my male guide was Joshua.

It was shortly after my exposure to my guides that I opened my mind to the power of energy within myself. I learned to meditate and incorporated the practice into every day of my life. But more on that—and Joshua and Leah—later.

I still have the cassette with the word *"Ian"* spelled out in red ink on the A side. It holds a special place in my mind as a turning point in my life, a moment when I opened up to a new, inner world of experience.

The experience with Louisa and Ian was the catalyst for me to expand my boundaries and learn of things I knew nothing about. As a dentist I attended copious hours of seminars and presentations, but they were all dealing with something I knew a lot about—the mouth. I set out to explore the world of "spirituality," and I had no idea what kind of an impact my search would have on me.

Now if I can just find a cassette player.

Turning Over a New Tree

"The sun at home warms better than the sun elsewhere."

~ Albanian Proverb

"If you go anywhere, even paradise, you will miss your home."

~ Malala Yousafzai

The stroke disrupted my internal body thermostat. As much as I loved Flagstaff and the clean mountain air it offered, it was difficult getting accustomed to the constant heat and smog of the desert valley. Automobiles were not tested and regulated for emissions at that time, and because the Phoenix valley covered a large geographic area and had no mass transit alternatives, most people drove everywhere. Auto emissions were a major contributor to the very poor air quality.

The opportunity to become an insurance professional and have a target market of dentists and doctors had allowed me to start another profession, one that I found I enjoyed and was good at.

Since my parents were in their seventies, and because I had a number of dental friends in Minnesota, I decided to move back to Minneapolis, Minnesota, after twenty years in Arizona.

The University of Minnesota is located in Minneapolis and contains departments of dentistry, medicine, pharmacy, nursing and veterinary practice, all of which provided me with an excellent potential source of insurance prospects. Shortly after moving I tested and received my Minnesota insurance license and, subsequently, studied and obtained my Series 6/63 securities licenses. This license allowed me to sell mutual funds and limited partnerships.

For the first eighteen months, as I established myself in the disability insurance industry, I worked out of my rented house. I was blessed to achieve the same kind of success selling insurance in Minnesota as I had working with medical professionals in Arizona. I had no trouble calling classmates—individuals who were in dental school when I attended—and any dentist listed in the telephone directory. I told them all the same thing: I wanted to make sure that what happened to me didn't happen to them and their families. Many of them responded to the messages I left with their receptionists.

I was considered an insurance "broker," which meant I could represent a number of different companies, as opposed to being a captive agent representing only one company. However, because one insurance company's policy was so superior for the medical professional (which was my target market) than any of the others, I ended up recommending its coverage to all of the prospects with whom I spoke. I only enrolled individuals with other companies when they either didn't qualify medically for the best policy or when they wanted a lower premium amount.

An interesting thing started happening in the course of meeting with prospective insurance clients (many of whom were friends or classmates). Oftentimes individuals would ask me to help them find an associate dentist or help them sell their dental practices. Minnesota is a very consumer protection-oriented state, and in order for an individual to sell any type of business opportunities, he or she must have a real estate license. So, out of a desire to help my friends/clients, I attended the classes and became a licensed real estate agent; after two years I tested and received my real estate broker license. With this in hand I could legally help dentists sell their practices, or help a busy dentist find an associate dentist to join his/her practice.

I had no way of knowing just how huge an impact my decision to become a "dental transition specialist" would have on my future.

I started a company called Transition Resources, Inc. There were a few other dental transition companies in Minnesota and I researched them all to be able to formulate a business strategy that would allow me to set myself apart from them. I added a tag line to the name Transition Resources, Inc.: "Specializing in Quality Practices and Quality People," and I had the words, *COMMUNICATION * INTEGRITY * RESULTS* printed on my business cards.

I had a little fun with the company logo design process as well. I enlisted the services of a graphic artist and had her make up twenty different designs for a logo for Transition Resources, Inc. I ruled out ten designs immediately, then sent the remaining ten designs to twenty of my clients and asked them to choose their favorite five designs. I waited a week for their responses and then tallied their results. I then sent the top five selections to the same twenty clients and asked them to choose their favorite logo. It happened to be the same one I personally chose. To this day when talking to those clients I still hear about the fun they had being a part of my company's logo design.

For years I wore many hats; those associated with being a fledgling insurance agent and the others being a fledgling "dental transition specialist." It was a busy time for me. I drove an average of 30,000 miles a year travelling all over the Midwest and meeting with insurance and/or transition clients. I went to Dallas, Texas, to attend a class teaching the complex methodology involved in formulating an accurate valuation of a dental practice. This tool—providing "practice" valuations to clients—was another valuable tool to add to my belt.

Sometime during my third year back in Minnesota my banker Bruce invited me to lunch. He also invited Joe, a principal of a respected CPA firm in Minneapolis, to join us. Bruce had told Joe I was working out of my house, doing everything involved with building two companies—including all the clerical work. Joe explained to me that his firm wanted to expand further into the dental market, and he invited me to work out of their office in downtown Minneapolis. The rent would be negligible and I'd have access to printing, copying and binding services, as well as a few hours of clerical help per week.

I accepted immediately. The offer was one of the nicest things that had happened to me since my stroke.

There was a further bonus beyond the office support. In my previous professional life as a practicing dentist I was around patients, friends and staff eight to ten hours a day. With my work since the stroke I was alone 95 percent of the time. Joe's offer was the perfect opportunity to be around people and enjoy the bustling energy of a busy metropolitan area. The fact is, I'm a people-person.

I loved the twelve-plus years I spent working out of the CPA firm and built some of my closest friendships in the firm. I left only because I was offered an office in an insurance agency representing the company I endorsed. I'd been the top disability insurance producer for that company in the Minneapolis-St. Paul area and was approached by the agency to join them. My new office was four blocks away from the CPA firm's offices, so the familiarity and friendships I had made remained strong. I referred a lot of clients to the CPA firm, and they in turn referred a number of transition clients to me. It was definitely a win/win arrangement.

***

I really found a calling as a "dental transition specialist." Although I had always felt tremendously rewarded being able to deliver the benefits of a disability policy to a disabled dentist, or the death benefits of a life insurance policy to a deceased's family, this new "gig" was different. At first I wondered why, but I soon realized that being a dental transition specialist made me feel so good because I typically dealt with happy people and happy families looking forward to their futures—as opposed to individuals receiving insurance benefits as a substitute for a profession or a deceased loved one.

Transition Resources became a nationally recognized transition firm. Again, my father's words echoed in my head: "Michael, your reputation follows you everywhere". I was very fortunate early on to have identified my "ideal client" ("quality people and quality practices"), and in most cases I didn't veer from that ideal.

In my initial meeting with a prospective dentist wanting to sell and retire I would always ask one question: "What do you want out of this transition?" Inevitably, my "ideal client" would say, "I want to make sure my patients and staff are well taken care of." Nowhere in that initial conversation was the amount of money they wanted from the sale mentioned.

I explained that I worked from an "abundance mentality"—meaning that in all transitions there was always more than enough for both parties, and my goal was to structure the transition so both parties would walk away from the closing table feeling good about what had just happened. Again, I was basically looking for win/win results.

The few times I veered from this "ideal" situation for one reason or another were the few times the transitions were either contentious in some way, or simply not as smooth as they could have been.

One of my fondest, if bittersweet, memories from this time is this: I received a long-distance phone call from a dentist named Paul who asked for help selling his practice as soon as possible. He had just been diagnosed with terminal cancer and had been given six months to live. Even with this scenario facing him, he still wanted to make sure his patients, staff and family were well taken care of. My heart sank for a moment given the timeline, but when I heard the peace in his voice, I calmly told him I would do everything possible to make his wishes a reality.

Normally it took nine months to two years to sell a practice outside of the metropolitan area. I worked hard to accelerate the process, and within five months we had reached a successful transition that worked well for everyone.

Paul passed away two months later. I sent my condolences to his widow and received the following beautiful card in response:

> *Dear Dr. Mike,*
>
> *Thank you for the card and your kind words of sympathy. A special thanks for all that you did to help Paul in his most difficult situation. The sale of the dental practice couldn't have gone any better. Paul and I are thankful for all of your help.*
>
> *Sincerely,*
> *Bonnie, Will & Nate*

Being able to help in situations like these was one of the greatest joys of my life.

Although I still do dental practice valuations for many reasons (divorce, practice sales, practice mergers, estate planning, etc.), I recently merged Transition Resources with another transition company. My reasons were simple: I wanted to slow down, I wanted to make sure my existing clients were well taken care of, and I wanted to spend more time in Arizona.

***

No discussion of my return to Minnesota would be complete if I didn't give a shout out to my old fraternity brothers and sisters.

You may recall that I joined the Delta Sigma Delta fraternity when I went to dental school fresh out of community college. When I moved back to Minnesota from Arizona I took over as the alumni director for the undergraduate Theta Chapter. Each year I helped a number of new graduates begin their careers by reviewing their employment agreements and finding dental practices for the few wanting to buy. I held this position for seventeen years.

The fraternity has been a very important and valuable part of my life. I've gotten to know fellow Delts from all over the world, and a number of the U.S. Delts have become very dear personal friends. Being a member of the fraternity has also been instrumental in the growth of both my disability insurance and dental transition specialist careers.

In this, my efforts to give back to a community that supported and inspired me turned into a huge win/win scenario for me and a many others.

So . . . Thank you, Delta Sigma Delta.

Be safe and happy, my Delt brothers and sisters!

Pam

"Clairvoyants can see flashes of colour, constantly changing in the aura that surrounds every person."

~ *Annie Besant*

About ten years after my stroke, I was asked to host a black-tie dinner in San Francisco, one honoring a good friend of mine who was being inducted as the president of an international organization. Because it was to be a black-tie event and I didn't want to go solo, I invited a dear friend who lived in southern California to be my guest. She could accompany me to the black-tie event and we could spend the rest of the time enjoying San Francisco. I hadn't seen her since her wedding over twenty years previous, but she was now divorced, and I looked forward to reconnecting with her and catching up on our lives.

We shared a marvelous weekend, and during the course of one of our conversations she mentioned a lady named Pam, whom she used as a personal spiritual advisor. She highly recommended Pam and suggested I call to set up an appointment.

I did just that soon after returning to Minnesota. Pam must have been in high demand, because the earliest appointment I could secure for a thirty-minute telephone appointment was four months down the road.

It was worth the wait: the telephone meeting was as eye-opening and remarkable as my experience with Louisa and Ian had been. Pam's gift was that she could visualize the energy colors surrounding an individual. These colors are known as one's "aura," and, surprisingly, the colors uncannily define a person's personality. Pam told me she was aware of her gift as a child and, until she found its benefits, attempted to be a successful professional businessperson. She spoke for twenty-five minutes and, as our thirty-minute session was winding down, I asked her what I should do next in my life.

She said she didn't know, but she told me of a client of hers from New York who had enrolled in a Masters in Spiritual Psychology program at the University of Santa Monica in California. This had provided him with tremendous satisfaction in his life. The two-year program was structured so students could attend classes one weekend a month for two years. This made it possible for students from long distances away to attend.

Something about this idea resonated deeply with me. My meeting with Pam was in February; by April that same year I had applied for and was accepted into the Masters in Spiritual Psychology program at the University of Santa Monica.

Interestingly enough, over the years I had several more meetings with Pam, a number of them in person and some via the telephone. Two years after our first meeting, and while I was attending the University of Santa Monica, I took a drive to meet with her in one of our face-to-face sessions. During our session Pam suddenly asked me:

"Who is Joshua? He's a smart aleck, isn't he?" and she laughed.

Her next statement surprised me even more: "Leah is the more powerful one of the two."

I had never mentioned Louisa, Ian, Joshua or Leah to Pam.

***

* Note: Because Pam's work has made such a positive impression in my life, I humbly offer a simple suggestion. If you're interested, **go to www.auracolors.com and take the Aura Colors Quiz. I think you'll be surprised at and enjoy the accuracy of the quiz results.** *If you choose to work with Pam, another positive aspect of doing so is that all of her sessions are recorded for the client's use and future review. Digital recordings of the sessions are emailed within twenty-four hours.*

PART II

THE JOURNEY OF A COACH

"Abundance is a process of letting go;
that which is empty can receive."

~ Bryant A. McGill

Spiritual Psychology

"Live as if you were to die tomorrow.
Learn as if you were to live forever."

~ Mahatma Gandhi

"The journey that I have undertaken, meeting people from
all walks of life and learning from them, has
been my biggest achievement."

~ Aamir Khan

The fifteen months I spent at the University of Santa Monica in the Masters in Spiritual Psychology program were some of the best months of my life.

The University was founded over three decades before, and one of the main lessons of its mission statement immediately spoke to me: "Always do the right thing, for the right reason, the right way." **Very simply, everything should be done from the heart, or in a heart-centered manner**. If you've read this far in my story you are probably not surprised that I immediately took to this way of thinking and feeling.

I was part of an amazing class made up of (to name a few) a judge, an attorney, several physicians, heirs to fortunes, professionals seeking alternate ways of doing things and a number of individuals from the movie industry.

I found early on that "spiritual psychology" was not religion-based. The 270 individuals in my class came from all over the world; they were from every religion I knew of, and some I had never heard of. The first day began with each student standing up and introducing him or herself. This was followed by an orientation covering the next two years' curriculum: what it would contain, estimated homework time expected of students and some background on the school and why it was founded. Students were given an extensive reading list of books that were to be mandatory reading, and the curriculum included term papers and other required work.

The Masters program at USM takes two years to complete. Students work through an accelerated curriculum condensing the coursework into one weekend a month for two years. This means students must commit a significant portion of their time to homework between those weekends.

My classes were held in a large auditorium with a raised stage in front and the entire class in attendance. At every meeting there was tremendous energy in the room. The majority of the first year's curriculum was spent learning different communication skills, like heart-centered listening, self-forgiveness, compassion, speaking and thinking without judgment and so on.

The teaching model was very unique. Students first spent time learning a communication skill. Following this teaching portion, students were encouraged to share experiences with that particular skill in their lives thus far. How had it worked for them? Could they see times in their past when it might have been helpful to communicate using one communication skill instead of another? Were there other times when they had had powerful success with a skill? We were made aware of—or had our feeling confirmed for us—that we were coming off two or three decades of the world being controlled by greed and that there was a global movement to make the world better by being a better person and paying it forward in some way. I was amazed how many of my classmates came from dysfunctional relationships or were recovering from substance abuse or eating disorders. In my opinion we all found our way to USM to find ways to make our lives more complete, to be better at what we did professionally, to be happier in our personal lives and to find ways to be better stewards of the Earth.

After the educational discussion and sharing we dispersed for a half-hour break, during which time the area was converted into ninety, three-chair groupings spaced out over the entire room.

When we returned, we were asked to organize into three-person groups called "trios," and to pick a group of chairs.

Two of the chairs were positioned face-to-face. The third faced the other two, so the layout was t-shaped. The person in Chair 1 became the counselor. Chair 2, directly across from the counselor, was for the client. The person in Chair 3, facing both the client and counselor, was deemed the neutral observer.

The goal of the exercise was to work on the communication skill taught earlier in the day. For a predetermined time (for example, five minutes), the client would begin talking about something that was bothering them, whether past or present. They could speak uninterrupted for the time allotted. At the end of that time, a light bell would ring, indicating the time was up. For the next block of time, the counselor, using the skill learned earlier, would attempt to help the client go deeper into the reason for their issue. When that time was up the bell would ring and the neutral observer addressed the counselor on what he/she did well, what they observed in the client's reactions, and so on. Then the bell would ring and . . . all three individuals would stand up and switch chairs. The counselor became the patient. The patient became the neutral observer. And the neutral observer became the counselor.

The Trio exchange happened regularly, usually twice a day. Students were dissuaded from meeting with the same trio partners and encouraged to find new people each time.

As might be expected, we got to know each other very well! The more we did the Trio process, the more we realized how powerful of a teaching tool it was. The release of pent-up feelings and emotions by individuals in the Client chair became common and accepted by all of us. To allow the affected classmate to complete his/her healing process, we were directed not to offer our support unless we were asked.

Of course, strict confidentiality was stressed; breaking it was grounds for dismissal from the program.

***

Securing a master's degree was not the main reason I attended the University of Santa Monica. I actually went there in the hope that I could obtain the answer to a question that had been on my mind for years. You may have asked it of yourself as well.

"Why am I really here?"

As far as I was concerned, completing the education and getting a degree would be icing on my cake—if I received the direction I was seeking.

Age-wise, I fell into the oldest 15 percent of the classmates, and throughout the first fifteen months I was asked a number of times by trio members if I'd ever considered being a life coach. I was sure their questions came about because I was an excellent listener. I also had enjoyed weaving the lessons I'd learned in my life into our discussions regarding the issues and needs of my fellow trio members. I felt very comfortable and at-home in the counselor chair, and I enjoyed learning and working on the communication skills while sharing them with classmates.

Oddly enough, despite the transformative power of my time at USM, I ended up having to make a decision that was one of the hardest of my life. Fifteen months into the program I informed the student liaison I had decided to leave the University of Santa Monica to become a certified life coach. The more I researched what a "life coach" does and the services they provide, the more certain I became that being a life coach was what I wanted to do in the next stage of my life. Knowing this, I decided to direct all of my energy towards becoming one.

I made (and kept) a number of wonderful friends at USM, and it was with sadness that I left—but with joy that I pursued becoming a certified life coach.

A Heart-Centered Existence

"The best and most beautiful things in the world cannot be seen or even touched—they must be felt with the heart."

~ Helen Keller

These days the communication skills I learned at USM are second nature to me. I carry with me the intention to live my life in the "authentic self" state of mind. A few years after leaving USM I was asked to train thirty new insurance agents on how I would approach prospective clients. Do you know how I did the training?

I separated the prospects into groups of three and used the trio method. I personally prepared and supplied the script to Chair 1. The results of the training were excellent, as each participant felt what a client might feel, and each realized the importance of observation as well.

I highly recommended the book *Loyalty to Your Soul*, by Drs. Ron and Mary Hulnick, to all of my coaching clients, and now I'll recommend it to you. Drs. Ron and Mary were my instructors and two of the founding members of the University of Santa Monica. It is an excellent book and chronicles in detail much of that amazing first-year curriculum.

What was my takeaway from USM?

It's hard to put it all into words, but briefly: I learned communication skills I didn't even know existed. I learned how to better use the communication skills I already had. I learned about my "authentic self," about how my "ego" fits into my life. I confirmed one thing I knew about myself: that I was an excellent listener. And of course I learned the importance of doing the right thing, the right way for the right reasons.

In short, I learned how to live a "heart-centered existence," and I feel grateful for the lessons and the wonderful friends I met along the way.

Meditation

"Meditation is painful in the beginning but it bestows immortal Bliss and supreme joy in the end."

~ *Swami Sivanda*

As I mentioned earlier, meditation has been a consistent part of my life for many years. I enjoy meditating, and my secrets to you for doing so as well are as follows:

- Don't work too hard at it
- Make it something you look forward to doing
- Don't take it too seriously
- Don't get discouraged

It may take a little time getting comfortable with achieving mental quietness, but once you achieve the feeling, it's yours to have forever. There are a number of online "how to meditate" sites or, if you learn by doing, you can find someone who teaches individuals to meditate.

Just remember, there is no such thing as "only one way to meditate." You'll find one that fits you perfectly and, shortly after you do, you'll wonder why you didn't learn to meditate sooner. Five minutes of mediation is a good goal starting out.

For my own part, I also wrap up my meditations with a short prayer, one of which goes like this:

Thank you for the abundance in every facet of my life.
Thank you for guiding me on my life's path.
Thank you for keeping me from evil and
for me not causing any pain.
Thank you for filling my life with love.

***

If you don't already meditate, I highly recommend learning how. Meditation has proven health benefits and it is a great way to achieve a good night's sleep. It offers a phenomenal way to start each day fresh with a clear mind, and it's also an excellent way to calm yourself in a heated moment during the day. What's more, over time it can lead to a greater understanding of yourself, your life, and the world around you.

Patience & Faith

"Have patience. All things are difficult before they become easy."

~ Saadi

Another practice you may find helpful in addition to meditation is writing down your desires. But just as important as writing them down is reading your list out loud; you'll probably find yourself editing the desires by changing the words you first used, and you'll find the list becomes more specific and accurate to what you really want.

Remember that not all desires or wishes are answered at the exact moment we would like them to be. The powers that be do not understand "24/7/365"—they're in their own timeframe.

Patience and believing your desires will manifest are your two required prerequisites. One of my favorite quotes comes from Wayne Dyer: *"Unlimited patience produces immediate results."*

You must have faith. At some time in my life I heard a definition of faith that resonated deep within me. I don't recall where or when I heard it but I've used it for many years:

"Faith is the ability to see the invisible
and believe in the impossible."

~ Unknown

Guides

"Your mind will answer most questions if you
learn to relax and wait for the answer."

~ *William S. Burroughs*

In an earlier chapter I talked about my harrowing helicopter ride with Jeremy and how I had received several "advance warnings" not to take it. In that instance those warnings came in the form of a tightening in my stomach.

When I was a practicing life coach, I coached my clients on how to listen to their own "guides." You might experience these guides as a voice in your head, a feeling in your stomach or even a sensation of someone grabbing your arm. Every one of us has a guide (call it what you'd like: intuition, spirit, uneasy feeling, etc.), but very few people either know how to "listen" to their guide, or know how to listen to the messages being conveyed to them.

Wouldn't it give you a tremendous peace of mind to know that someone/something is looking out for you and trying to protect you from making terrible mistakes? It's not that hard to come by this feeling.

In my case, ever since I learned about their existence, I've listened to Joshua and Leah. Before I was aware of them, however, I usually didn't "listen to my gut" in either business or personal decisions, and I have the battle scars to show for some poor decisions.

So even if you don't feel "connected" to your guides, remember the lesson about paying attention to your gut feelings. No matter how good something looks, if it doesn't feel right . . . walk away.

***

As mentioned previously, I've meditated daily for over thirty years, sometimes twice a day (to start my day after waking and to end it before going to bed at night). Over a period of two years I attended the Berkeley Psychic Institute in Berkeley, California, for a continuum of three separate series of classes: Meditation 1, 2, 3, Healing 1 and 2; and Clairvoyance. I had to take Meditation 1, 2 and 3 and Healing 1 and 2 before I could take the Clairvoyance class. All of the classes were interesting, and the external appearances of my classmates were *extremely* interesting (I was the only one who didn't have at least one visible piercing or tattoo).

Meditation 1 was entitled "Meditation for Kindergarteners," and I found it both enjoyable and simple. Since I alternate my mediations frequently, I frequently use the Kindergartener as one of the alternate techniques.

No matter what technique I employ, thanking Joshua and Leah for their presence and guidance is part of the ending of every meditation.

Only in Berkeley

In getting ready to go back to Minnesota after a session at the Berkley Psychic Institute, I was in a public Berkeley coin laundry facility folding my clean underwear for my trip back the next day. I looked up from folding to see a unique man staring at me from across the table. He stood about 5'10", weighed about 135 pounds, and didn't have an exposed piece of skin that wasn't tattooed. Both earlobes were stretched to accommodate large black circular stones, his nose sported a ring through the septum and both of his eyebrows were graced with piercings. He was dressed in a black sleeveless t-shirt, skinny black pants and black boots, and from the odor he emitted I deduced he hadn't showered in a while.

"Can I have a pair of your underwear?" he asked.

His question caught me by surprise. I folded the last piece of laundry, smiled at him, wished him good luck, picked up my laundry bag and nodded as I walked onto the sidewalk. I walked about half a block and thought to myself, "He probably could really use a pair of underwear, and I could go without one pair," so I turned around and walked back to the laundry. The man dressed like Zorro or Johnny Cash was still inside; I handed him a pair of my REI athletic boxer shorts.

He held them up and asked, "Do you have another style?"

I couldn't believe what I'd just heard, and I laughed. I politely took them from his hand, shook my head and said, "Only in Berkeley."

A Lifecoaching Lesson about Ego & the Authentic Self

"Authenticity soothes the soul."

~ Arthur P. Ciaramicoli

Why is it that young children don't get stage fright? Why do they sleep soundly at night and laugh so easily?

When we're born and brought into this world, we come without any baggage—we are innocent of any preconceived ideas and inquisitive about everything. In short, we are truly "authentic" and pure as youngsters.[6]

What happens to that purity as we get older?

There is an energy within us, an element of our personality, that uses our inquisitive nature to develop. For lack of a better

---

[6] Disclaimer: I'm not including the unfortunate children who, as young and malleable individuals, are exposed to trauma, abuse and all other negative external forces. I'm referencing the vast majority of children who grow up normal and healthy.

name, and because everyone has heard the word, let's call this energy "ego."

Every one of us has an ego but it's the level of control it has over us (or that we have over it) that determines whether we have a positive or negative ego. Ego never stops trying to control how we react. When we react negatively to a stimulus, ego wins, and each time it wins, it grows in power. Ego uses tactics like fear, judgment, coveting, confidence, etc., to strengthen its control—all the while making us think it's acting in our best interest. It is my opinion that a negative ego uses the tactics listed above to become stronger and thus gain more control over an individual.

The ego's tentacles are constantly reaching out to grab negative suggestions or acts of parents, teachers, relatives, media, etc., to use as ammunition to gain control over our personality and the way we respond to future challenges.

When we don't accept accountability, our ego is winning.

When we practice self-pity, our ego is winning.

When we covet a wealthy colleague's assets, our ego is winning.

When we judge why someone does something, our ego is winning.

When we worry about something over which we have no control, our ego is winning.

A beautiful thing is the fact that the ego can be a non-factor if it doesn't have the power to affect our actions/desires. The secret to making the ego a non-factor is recognizing your "authentic self" and achieving the state of mind it provides. The "authentic self" is simply one's being, void of ego's control. More simply, think of the "authentic self" as your best friend and your ego as a two-faced acquaintance. Once you realize the existence of ego—how it acts and what it is trying to do—and see how finding your authentic self can defeat the efforts of the ego, your life can become wonderful. You can look at past conflicts and worries without dredging up emotions and regrets about them again, and you can laugh at yourself while completely disregarding your ego.

If you were blessed to have had supportive parents and teachers, as I was, the chances are excellent that you can keep your ego in check. However, having it in check is not as powerful as controlling it. Recognizing and acknowledging your authentic self will enhance your life by minimizing the strength of your ego.

Remember: the ego wants control. By acknowledging the authority of your authentic self you usurp the power of the ego.

***

I taught my clients about the presence of the ego, and about the negative power it can wield. I then shared with them how to recognize and embrace their authentic self and engage with the freedom that comes from doing so.

In most cases, this is not an easy learning process. The ego has had many years to solidify its control. It will try to convince you of how foolish embracing the authentic self is, and it will do its best to make you believe it knows best.

The process I shared is as follows, step by step:

1. Acknowledge the existence of your authentic self (usually this takes the most time).

2. Identify with and embrace your authentic self.

3. Strengthen the bond with it.

4. Acknowledge the existence of your ego.

5. Realize the control it has.

6. Take control away from the ego by introducing it to your authentic self.

7. Continually acknowledge and embrace your authentic self in every instance of indecision. The more you do this, the less power the ego has, and the happier and stronger you will become.

Again, Step 1 is the most difficult part of the process but, once you achieve it, Steps 2 through 6 are simple and enjoyable. The reason acknowledging the existence of your authentic self is so difficult is twofold. First, the *authentic self* is a completely foreign concept, which makes accepting its existence more difficult. Second, ego will resist losing control over you from the second you want to change for the better.

But it will have to yield once you realize that your authentic self exists.

Getting to know your authentic self and living within it is a wonderful way to be. When you live as your authentic self you'll find you don't have the extreme highs or lows you're accustomed to experiencing in your daily life. You'll smile more often than ever before. You won't worry about things that used to bother you. What's more, you'll find that people enjoy being around you more than ever because, in short, you radiate positive, loving energy when living an authentic-self existence.

***

Living life as your authentic self is the most beautiful feeling in the world.

What Is a Life Event Loop (LEL)?

"It is seldom in life that one knows that a coming event is to be of crucial importance."

~ Anya Seton

Individuals consult singing coaches to learn to sing better, batting coaches to learn to hit a curve ball, ballet coaches to learn a difficult dance move, and so on. Given this, doesn't it make sense to hire a life coach to help with life problems?

Life coaches aren't supposed to give advice, even if the solution to a problem seems obvious. They're trained instead to ask questions, the answers to which empower clients to seek out solutions themselves. When a client experiences an "aha moment" leading to happiness, it is a milestone that builds trust and respect between client and coach. Usually it only takes one such "aha moment" to make a client look forward to their next coaching session.

As a life coach myself (without all the answers) I was constantly striving to improve my understanding of things, and I sought out educational opportunities wherever I could find them, just as I did when practicing dentistry so many years ago. I utilized the services of my own life coach for many years. Most life coaches have their own coach and consult them often.

I once attended a seminar in Denver, Colorado, where the presenter spoke of a **clinical psychologist by the name of Dr. Dory Hollander, whose entire practice was made up of executives who were either "burning out" or already "burned out" in their current positions.** Even though I couldn't personally picture spending all of my time dealing with unhappy people, I found the presentation very interesting. I took copious notes and thought that maybe someday I might be able to apply them to something of value.

Over the years the lessons I learned resonated in different areas, and I finally realized that the psychologist's observations and treatments could be applied in almost *every* scenario, ranging from childhood experiences to personal relationships to family dynamics to professional interactions—and everything in between. I ended up developing a strategy based on Dr. Hollander's techniques that became a very valuable tool for me in my coaching business. I named my process *Life Event Loop*, and its methodology can be explained with the use of the four following grids.

This tool can be applied to any new situation or relationship. Let's look at the first grid (page 144). As you can see, there are four quadrants, each one indicating a distinct stage of a scenario. **Every relationship starts in Quadrant I, moves to Quadrant II, then to Quadrant III and finally to Quadrant IV**. On the top of the grids are the words **"Like"** and **"Don't Like,"** and on the left side are the words (from the bottom up) **"Not Comfortable"** and **"Comfortable."**

Let's see how the loop works and, as an example, let's use the scenario of a relationship, from beginning to end, with someone to whom you're attracted. Along the way, we'll also consider the quadrants in career terms.

Quadrant I

First you start in Quadrant I. You "like" what you see in this other person, but you're "not comfortable." Let's say you've just seen the person and find them appealing, but like most of us in such a situation you probably feel some combination of **"anxious," "challenged," or "uptight**." Will *they* like *you*? How should you approach them? Even after the first few successful dates that anxiety may remain as the relationship finds its "feet" and slowly, hopefully, begins to feel more comfortable. Quadrant I represents a time when insecurities rise to the surface and you wonder if you'll be able to move the relationship to the next level—or in the terms of our discussion, to the next Quadrant.

Note, too, that you would be experiencing similar feelings in a new job. Will you be able to pull it off or will you fall flat on your face? What do you need to figure out to reach the point where you feel "settled in"?

The length of time an individual stays in Quadrant I varies, but it's usually around six to twelve months.

	Like	Don't Like
Comfortable	**II**	**III**
Not Comfortable	Anxious Challenged Uptight **I**	**IV**

Quadrant II

The normal progression is to go from Quadrant I to Quadrant II. Quadrant II is the "ideal" time and, in an ideal world, the place anyone would like to stay. In terms of the relationship we talked about above, you're comfortable and happy to be with the individual. This isn't just a "honeymoon" phase, though that can be part of it. It's also where you're generally happy and satisfied with the state of the relationship. The same applies if we're talking about a job—you've gotten over the initial learning curve that made you feel uncomfortable and perhaps incompetent, and you now know what you're doing and enjoy doing it.

	Like	Don't Like
Comfortable	Happy Satisfied **II**	**III**
Not Comfortable	Anxious Challenged Uptight **I**	**IV**

You might think that in a perfect world you could stay in Quadrant II forever. It might seem ideal to have no change or stress. But realistically, without change or stress there would be no growth. And without growth, people tend to become stagnant and unhappy. Why is that? Let's pause a moment in our review of the quadrants to explore that question.

Stress vs. Distress

There are really *two* types of stress: *stress* and *distress.*

Let's first look at **positive stress**, the kind that supports growth. Not surprisingly, I like to think of it in terms of an analogy drawn from dentistry.

An orthodontist actually uses "stress" to (slowly!) move teeth around an individual's mouth in order to achieve the perfect bite and smile. Each tooth is surrounded by dense bone in the jaw. In order to move a tooth in a specific direction, *stress*—in the form of force from an orthodontic bracket with wire going through it—is put on the tooth. Under this stress, the bone towards which the tooth is being pulled will gradually break down, and the tooth will move into this area of bone loss. At the same time, *new* bone will grow in the area the tooth is being pulled *away from*, filling in the gap where the tooth used to be.

To avoid causing damage to the roots of the teeth, the wires are changed frequently and the teeth are moved very slowly. This is why a normal orthodontic procedure will take between two to three years.

Once every tooth is in an ideal position, the patient is instructed to wear a retainer. This serves to keep the teeth in place by spreading the stress (force) evenly over all of the teeth while the bone strengthens around them. In other words, the retainer applies *good stress* to the new arrangement of teeth, thereby maintaining the results of the orthodontic procedure.

This is a perfect analogy for how to use positive stress for growth and development. In a healthy life, stress is needed to grow. Everyone becomes stronger and grows by working through stressful situations. The "trick" is to control that stress so it supports and encourages your development. Stress can be controlled by a number of ways; examples would be strenuous exercise, yoga or meditation, a book or coffee club, and so on.

Distress, on the other hand, is **bad stress**, and it is usually caused by our old friend, *ego.* Distress can cause sleeplessness, eating disorders, and substance abuse. Without professional intervention it can be difficult or impossible to control. Examples of *distress* in action include frequent anger, short tempers, distrust in oneself or others, rumor-mongering, envy and coveting.

Mistrust is a strong catalyst for *distress*. Mistrust leads to speculation and judging others, which, taken together, can be devastating to a personal or professional relationship.

Growth is vital to our well being. Growth caused by stress is one of the main reasons an individual can't stay in Quadrant II forever. The only thing guaranteed in life is . . . *change*, and change is usually preceded by some form of stress. Stress makes it impossible to stay in Quadrant II forever. However, one's ability to get back to or remain in the authentic self state will both minimize the stress and shorten the time it will take an individual to get back to Quadrant II. Or, in the case of a new relationship or job, shorten the time between Quadrant I and Quadrant II.

The time an individual spends in Quadrant II can be anywhere between six to twelve months and thirty-plus years. When individuals start getting bored and frustrated with their partner or job, they move into Quadrant III.

Quadrant III

In Quadrant III one is still good at and comfortable doing what they were doing in Quadrant II, but now they're not enjoying it as much. The relationship may still be "good"—it may meet most needs and "fit" like a comfortable glove—but dissatisfaction is creeping in from the sidelines.

	Like	Don't Like
Comfortable	Happy Satisfied **II**	Frustrated Bored **III**
Not Comfortable	Anxious Challenged Uptight **I**	**IV**

Common side effects of doing something one's good at but not having *fun* at include frustration and boredom. These same symptoms occur in personal relationships as well, as do thoughts of whether the relationship is strong and whether perhaps "wandering off the reservation" is in order to test it. So at home, starting to look elsewhere for sexual gratification and not finding pleasure in your activities with your significant other indicate a shift from Quadrant II to III. At work, being late to meetings and not following through on deadlines are two examples of being in

Quadrant III. And once you've made this change, moving from Quadrant III to Quadrant IV usually doesn't take very long.

Quadrant IV

An individual in Quadrant IV is unhappy and miserable and, in most cases, no longer comfortable with what they're doing—and they don't like doing it anymore. This often happens after someone spends too long at the same job, but it can also include, for example, a CEO who resigns from one corporation and takes up a similar position at another corporation. They often find themselves feeling dissatisfied again within a short period of time. This is because, unbeknownst to them, they move from Quadrant I to Quadrant IV very quickly, spending little time in Quadrant II. The "new" work is too similar to their old job, and the old feelings of dissatisfaction quickly flood back in.

Such individuals were the market of Dr. Hollander, mentioned in the opening of this chapter.

In relationship terms, an individual who finds him or herself in a marriage or partnership that has lost its joy and comfort, and which now consistently produces the opposite effects in his or her life, has entered Quadrant IV. That same individual, like the CEO above, may go from marriage to marriage to marriage, not understanding what the problem really is.

	Like	Don't Like
Comfortable	Happy Satisfied **II**	Frustrated Bored **III**
Not Comfortable	Anxious Challenged Uptight **I**	Unhappy Miserable **IV**

Personally, in my job journey after my stroke, I was in Quadrant I in each of my job endeavors for a short time. But because I approached all of the new jobs in the same way I approached my dental practice, I moved on to Quadrant II quickly. That is, I made the effort to quickly bring myself up to speed on what I needed to do to be competitive, which made me quickly feel comfortable and adept at the work. I also believed in what I was doing and the products I was selling, and this added to my sense of satisfaction with the work. What's more, I didn't stay in any of the jobs long enough to enter Quadrants III or IV.

Once I entered the insurance industry, my time in Quadrant I was very minimal (less than a month). I feel blessed that my time in Quadrant II lasted over twenty years before I decided to pass the service of my clients on to an individual whom I mentored for three years and consider a good friend. I never entered Quadrants III or IV.

Spending Time in Quadrant II

It's obvious from the diagrams above that Quadrant II is where most individuals would like to reside as much as possible. However, without knowledge of the Loop and the Quadrants, long-term happiness may seem unattainable. One of the values of understanding career and life stages in terms of these quadrants is that it enables you to recognize the signs of dissatisfaction early on; this can give you greater control over your own life and career.

We have seen in our brief discussion of stress why expecting to stay in Quadrant II *permanently* is unrealistic and, in terms of personal growth and development, undesirable. But even after accepting the fact that movement through all four quadrants is a necessary and valuable part of life, returning to and remaining for a time in Quadrant II after transitional periods is rather simple—and an essential part of a happy life.

A list of the ways to reach or stay present in Quadrant II more often could fill an entire book but, depending on individual scenarios, only a few would really be needed.

On that list would be (in no particular order):

1. Refocusing on what attracted you to the person or job in the first place

2. Learning a new technique or program in your current status, thus stimulating "good stress"

3. Learning to do something you've always wanted to do (e.g., play a musical instrument, or do photography, woodworking, cross-stitching, yoga, etc.)

4. Starting or reinstituting a weekly date night with your significant other

5. Learning about your heritage

6. Starting or resuming an exercise regimen, only this time with a goal (e.g., a five-kilometer run)

7. Volunteering your services to a charitable organization (many times there is a tremendous amount of self-satisfaction realized in helping others less fortunate)

8. Getting in touch with your authentic self

9. Seeking professional help (and being brave enough to do so)

10. Learning to meditate

The Element

There's another book I recommended to all of my coaching clients: *The Element*, by Dr. Ken Robinson. *The Element* addresses not only finding one's passion, but also what to do when you find it. The book is full of fascinating insights and questions to explore, many of which I suspect will resonate with you, as they have for my clients and for myself.

For example, there is no cookie-cutter, one-size-fits-all plan to ensure happiness and success. Dr. Robinson doesn't believe college after high school is for everyone. He provides short biographies of well-known, high-profile individuals who either didn't go to college or who left college before graduating. Chapter Five is entitled "Finding Your Tribe," and it points out that once one surrounds him or herself with individuals who think and enjoy the same things they do, they've found their Tribe, and the opportunities to shine and be happy surround them as they thrive in a supportive environment.

Overall, the book is a reminder that life is a journey with many different paths to take, and it's up to the individual to find the one that suits them best.

Burnout Leads to Burnout

"Leadership is an active role; 'lead' is a verb. But the leader who tries to do it all is headed for burnout, and in a powerful hurry."

~ Bill Owens

My first niche market as a life coach was working with medical professionals who were experiencing some phase of "burnout" in either their professional or personal lives. I spent hours researching the topic of burnout in the medical profession, and the research validated what I suspected. Physician burnout is a well-documented problem addressed extensively in medical periodicals.

However, nowhere did I find opinions or protocols on how burnout could be prevented or treated.

This lack of information on how burnout should be treated fueled my desire to be of assistance. I was very excited, thinking my services would be welcome and in high demand.

I learned quickly that I was completely wrong.

My services were not nearly as welcomed as I had hoped. After a little over a year working with burning-out or burned-out physicians, I realized that my trying to help them was actually affecting me negatively. I wasn't sleeping well, and certain individuals and their situations would remain in my thoughts well after a session. My own frustration was hitting me the hardest; it came from knowing I could help someone but not being allowed to convince *them* of that fact.

I had one basic rule in life coaching: I can probably help you, but I require complete truthfulness and honesty. I shared this rule and its follow-up rule—two untruths and you're out—in my first complementary session with every prospective client.

At the time I was engaged in this specific work, I knew "ego" had a strong foothold in the medical profession, but I didn't realize how overworked and underappreciated medical professionals were. Strong egos, mixed with a loss of control over the way they were forced to practice medicine, made for many unhappy individuals. Too often they would respond to a question about how they were handling this stress and intensity with an answer that made them look good (and, sadly, which fueled their egos), rather than answering honestly.

In other words, they were burned out, but acknowledging that fact—and working to change it—was not something their egos would let them do.

I have learned that trying to help people who won't help themselves is not only a losing battle, it's one that affects me negatively as well. So after politely telling the sixth physician that due to his untruthfulness we would no longer be working together, I realized it was time to change niche markets.

After the negative experience of coaching unhappy physicians, I changed my coaching niche to one in which I was working with individuals and businesses needing assistance in making decisions. I found the different ways people approached making important decisions in their lives to be fascinating. Some clients were very focused on making decisions based on financial gains. One client prioritized the best interest of the environment. Another client's decision involved how to best distribute their wealth to future heirs. I enjoyed working with these and other clients. I particularly appreciated those clients who simply saw the value in input from a neutral individual when making an important decision. I again found tremendous value in using the communications skills I learned at USM. In my initial meeting with prospective coaching clients I briefly explained heart-centered thinking, always doing so in a non-confrontational manner and allowing as many questions as needed to get the concepts across and help people feel comfortable with them. I found that most of my clients were open to including heart-centered thinking in their decision-making processes.

After the first few clients realized wonderful results in their decisions by avoiding simple issues—such as pre-judging their counterparts—I knew my new niche would be both valuable and fun going forward. My coaching style and methods might have been different than other coaches' techniques, but they were successful and enjoyable.

Nowadays, coaching is more of a hobby for me. I don't advertise my services, and I only work with referrals. I simply enjoy my life; coaching has been a wonderful part of it.

***

Life is too short not to work with individuals who make you happy.

Patsy and Booker

"All his life he tried to be a good person. Many times, however, he failed. For after all, he was only human. He wasn't a dog."

~ Charles M. Schulz

When growing up, our house was too small to have a pet. X also pretended she didn't like animals. I say "pretended" because after my sisters became married adults, they both had dogs. Posie had two dogs, Muffles and Muffin, two cute little Lhasa Apso/Cockapoo mixed siblings. Toot had Patches, a beautiful German Shepard. We would catch mom secretly petting and slipping the dogs treats, but she'd always feign disliking animals.

I am very fortunate that dogs like and are attracted to me, and I've always loved them. Because I have long been single, had an active lifestyle and done many things on the spur of the moment, I never thought it would be smart to own a dog. It wouldn't be fair to the dog but, just as importantly—and selfishly—I didn't want to be tied down either. I enjoyed dogsitting for friends, but I also enjoyed being able to go skiing or fishing or to stay overnight somewhere other than home when invited. In short, I had the best of both worlds.

***

Many years after the stroke, and at the close of my insurance career, I reconnected via phone with Patsy, a dear friend from Flagstaff. She was widowed and split her time between Arizona in the winter and Kentucky during the summer. We made a plan to meet for dinner and we both looked forward to seeing each other again. I wondered if she still had the infectious laugh and sense of humor I remembered so well.

As usual for me, I arrived at the restaurant early and noted there were a number of tables and a couple of booths unoccupied. Rather than asking to be seated, I reserved a booth and waited to the side of the front door. Would I recognize Patsy? Would she recognize me? Hell, it had been almost thirty years.

When she walked in the door I said, "Hey, Patsy." Tears filled her eyes and the thirty plus years seemed like a week. As we hugged I felt something brushing against my shin. I looked down and saw a young, jet-black lab looking up at me with large dark-brown eyes. He wore a yellow "SERVICE DOG IN TRAINING" cape on his back. He was attached to a leash, the other end of which was held by Patsy. She introduced me to him; his name was Booker.

When the hostess told us to follow her, I followed Patsy and Booker and smiled at Booker's distinctive Labrador waddle. Patsy and I were seated and Booker situated himself under the table, curled up in a ball beneath Patsy. Patsy explained she was a volunteer for Canine Companions for Independence, an organization that bred and trained service dogs to be companions for individuals suffering from a number of physical and emotional impairments, including military veterans suffering from Post-Traumatic Stress Disorder. Patsy was to have Booker for the first fifteen months of his life and socialize him, giving him the standard housetraining and taking him everywhere she went: airplanes, grocery stores, theaters, outdoor art festivals, and, of course, restaurants. She also took him to weekly obedience and command training classes.

Patsy had always loved animals. She now had horses and her own dogs and cats, and she felt this calling to be a volunteer was healing for her following the tragic passing of her husband. Booker was six months old and he was Patsy's first trainee. Booker was an English Lab—English labs are slightly smaller than American labs and have blockier heads and shorter ears than their American counterparts. They're also known to be mellower than American labs.

Booker laid at Patsy's feet as she and I spent almost two hours catching up on our lives and the friends we shared in common. When the dessert we ordered to share arrived, she asked why I was smiling. I softly told her to stand up and look over my edge of the booth. Booker had quietly left his spot at Patsy's feet and had his head in my lap; those big brown eyes were closed.

I was smitten.

"I want Booker!" I said to Patsy, only half-jokingly.

She laughed. "You can't have him!" Then a thoughtful look crossed her face. "But, you know, if you're serious, you *could* submit adoption papers for him. If he doesn't complete the final training at the service dog academy, maybe we can work something out."

She explained that there was usually a long list of individuals wanting to adopt the soon-to-be service dogs, but that the dogs' trainers—in Booker's case, her—had the first option to adopt out the dogs they trained. In the event Booker didn't complete his training and I wasn't high enough on the adoption list, having Patsy adopt Booker and then me buying him from Patsy could be a great option.

I downloaded, completed and faxed the adoption form that night, using Patsy's name as a reference.

A year later I was on my way to a fly-fishing trip to Montana when I received a call on my cell phone. Tonya from Canine Companions for Independence was on the other end of the line, and she reminded me of my submission of adoption papers for Booker.

"That's right," I said after a brief moment while the memory floated back up into consciousness.

"He's yours, if you want him."

I started shaking and pulled my car over.

Decision time! Then I remembered the way Booker seemed to have chosen *me* that night at dinner with Patsy

Do you, Michael, I asked myself, *agree to give up your impetuous freedom and become the proud owner of the "most beautiful boy in the world?"*

My decision and answer were quick, "Of course I want him! How much do I owe you and where do I have to go to get him?"

"Five-hundred dollars, and we're in Ohio."

My heart sank for a moment. "I'm on my way to Montana for a week. Can I get you a check in the mail as soon as I'm home?"

"Not a problem," said Tonya, and the relief flooded in. Then she added, "Congratulations!"

I hung up and turned to Pete, my fishing partner, where he sat in the passenger seat.

"It looks like I'm gonna be a dad soon—and I can't wait."

He gave me a confused look.

I called Patsy. It turned out she already knew Booker had become available. She was, in fact, hoping I still wanted him. She was in Kentucky and told me she would drive up to Ohio to pick Booker up. When convenient, I could take a road trip to visit her and pick up my "boy."

And what fine piece of luck had gotten him booted from the academy—and thereby into my life? He had been dismissed for getting distracted by little kids and little dogs; the temptation had been too great! Officially he was "too playful."

Not the best trait for a seeing-eye dog, I guess, but just fine for me.

After fifteen months of socializing Booker, Patsy had to take him to the Academy in Ohio and give him back. She told me it was one of the hardest things she'd ever had to do. Ironically the day she turned him in happened to be her birthday.

On the other hand, the day I picked up Booker at her house was exactly thirty years after my stroke.

My life was about to change—and for the better.

Love–But in a Totally Unexpected Way

"There is only one happiness in this life, to love and to be loved."

~ George Sand

Now, without going into any great detail I will say that there has been no shortage of trysts, hookups and dates in my life, and I've had a lot of wonderful female companionship. In particular I've been blessed to have four beautiful, long-term relationships with four amazing women. Close friendships remain with all of them, and I'm good friends with the spouses of two of them. (The other two are divorced from their first husbands, and one has remarried.)

Three of these relationships fell prey to timing and a rebound from a divorce, but one relationship clearly broke up because I've never had a strong paternal instinct. Put simply, I've never felt the urge to have children. Keeping my surname going through future generations has not been a powerful enough motivation to get married and have children.

(In fairness, if the four ladies in question were asked, the differences in the way men and women think, coupled with the fact there are always two sides to every story, might result in different explanations for why the relationships ended.)

As far as the paternal instinct question goes, I have five godsons, three beautiful nieces and one wonderful grandniece, who is also my goddaughter. I treasure all of them and have been an active part in many of their lives.

But now I'm also known as "Booker's Dad."

Booker is my first dog, and it took me the better part of our first six months together to get used to the fact he depends on me for everything.

I'm sure it took him a while to get used to me, too.

I had never experienced the unconditional love a dog can provide; now I experience it 24/7 when we're together. And, since all I have to do to receive that unconditional love is provide him with the basic things he needs—food, shelter and medical care—I think I'm getting a great deal. My love and joy are free for him to enjoy.

If he wants something, his tail wags from side-to-side, but if he's *really* happy his tail wags in big circles. For example, if I'm gone for any period of time, be it thirty minutes or four hours, when he hears the door open he greets me with his tail wagging in big circles and with two baby sneezes. When I return from a few days or a week away, you can add running in circles to the above actions. Friends or relatives who watch him when I'm away tell me he recognizes the sound of my car when I pull into their driveways and he bolts to the door to wait.

Booker has taught me how to love unconditionally. Throughout the course of a normal day, every time I pass him I either pet him, stroke his coat if he's lying down, or ruffle his ears—all of which I love doing. Sometimes he responds by looking up with his big brown eyes, but most often he'll roll on his back and wait for me to rub his stomach. Everything he does makes me smile. We walk four to five miles in two or three walks, seven days a week, rain or shine. While walking, I verbally communicate situations I'm trying to figure out (as if he understands). I can imagine how strange I must appear talking to a dog as I walk and he prances next to me. Periodically, he acknowledges me by cocking his head and looking up at me, but most of the time he's sniffing or peeing on something.

Except for one room, my entire house is tiled; watching him navigate a corner while running on the tile is definitely worth the price of admission—he looks like a car spinning its tires as it takes a corner at high speed. I use the carpeted room for exercising and stretching. Each morning, I quietly tip-toe to the carpet to stretch while he's sleeping in one of his sleeping areas with his head cocked to the side, his eyes rolled back and all four of his legs in the air. I'm there for five or ten minutes before I hear the sound of dog toenails coming across the tile.

I know what comes next. He enters and I say, "Well, good morning, buddy!" He does his two big dog stretches, two yawns and two baby sneezes, licks my face and curls up right next to me. If I haven't completed a specific stretch, I'll tell him to get up and move over so I can have more room, and he'll move. I'll continue the exercise and, in a short time, I'll feel a paw on my arm and dog breath on my face—he has returned to his original position, only this time closer. I've learned it's his way of saying he's ready for breakfast and our morning walk.

He's trained me well.

Studies show that petting a dog can lower blood pressure and be both therapeutic and relaxing. Therapy dogs are used in courtrooms to calm children who are testifying, and in mental wards to calm irritated patients. Many prisons are tasking life-sentence inmates to train dogs to be used as therapy dogs for the public, and many of these hardened criminals are reduced to tears when they have to return the dogs they've trained. Booker could easily fill all of these roles; calmness and love are natural parts of his demeanor.

Booker goes with me almost everywhere. Our walks are both beneficial and fun for each of us, and, right now, I can't picture my life without him in it. I realize we both hit the lottery when we were brought together. He got the master any dog would love. And me? Well, one of my affirmations after meditating came to fruition: "Thank you for filling my life with love."

Booker wasn't the "love" I expected. But I am so grateful for the way it turned out, and I gladly accept the gift of Booker's love. I know he will be in my life for a limited time, and for that reason I start every morning off with an affirmation: "I choose to make this day a special day for Booker and me."

What's more, I know that my affirmation—"Thank you for filling my life with love"—is still open and will be filled again.

I invite you to look around you and reflect on the gifts of love that are present in your own life right now. If something inspires you, express your gratitude for it/them, and consciously welcome more love into your life.

Personally, I'm looking forward to accepting the next gift of love that is brought to me.

Learning to Receive: Concluding Thoughts

"Asking is the beginning of receiving. Make sure you don't go to the ocean with a teaspoon – at lease take a bucket so the kids won't laugh at you."

~ *Jim Rohn*

Thank you for sharing with me some of the life events I've experienced and lessons I've learned along my life's journey. The unexpected benefit I received in writing this was that I actually learned a lot about myself. I realized I am a fighter and a survivor and I hold within myself vast amounts of humility and empathy for others. I've learned I am a "connector"; that is, I enjoy putting people together with other people, or putting people together with causes. I especially enjoy being able to share a personal experience when the sharing helps another avoid or navigate around a bad experience of their own. I take nothing for granted. I appreciate everyone I choose to be around and I make the most of every situation. I'm definitely not co-dependent and I don't require having a lot of people around me to be happy (having Booker around may be the reason for that).

For many years I believed the world was made up of two types of people: givers and receivers, with neither type being right or wrong.

I know for a fact that I am a giver. For example, one of the things I treasured most while in a committed relationship was, when I was out of town, being able to purchase a unique gift and surprise my partner by giving it to her at an unexpected moment. Seeing her eyes light up and feeling the warmth of the hugs and kisses that followed were treasured. I also have always loved being able to give to others through service and, as I say above, to bring people together. I love being a giver.

I had never been a good receiver. The stroke affected my confidence, and for many years I felt uncomfortable even accepting a compliment. The inability to accept kudos was very apparent in my stroke rehabilitation. Often, when I received compliments from therapists on my progress, I would find myself transferring my progress back to them by saying things such as, "Yes, but I wouldn't have been able to do that without your help."

While at the University of Santa Monica I shared my hesitancy and avoidance of receiving as a shortcoming and worked on it in a trio. It wasn't until one of my trio members said, "Michael, do you realize that by receiving, you're allowing someone the opportunity to give?" that I realized what I had been missing. That question and the impact it had on me actually changed the fullness of my life.

Over the past five years the effects of participating in extreme sports in my younger days have caught up with me and resulted in a knee replacement followed by a shoulder replacement (remember the skiing story with Boz?). Now I'm comfortable asking for help when I need to lift something above my shoulders, and the comfort comes from knowing that if our roles were reversed, the person I'm asking would ask me for help—and I would be pleased to be able to give it.

In the chapter about Richie I shared what became the signature for my personal emails. I've changed my email signature a few times over the years but I always seem to come back to this one . . .

Yesterday is a canceled check,

Tomorrow is a post-dated check,

Live today and . . .

Always love.

As I said, I've come to realize the signature is actually my life's philosophy. I've recited it when I needed reassurance. It brings me the clarity I need in times of challenge and it has provided me encouragement to move forward in accepting my journey. It's how I live.

I would like to offer you a few more parting thoughts drawn

from the previous pages. They may spark an impulse to reread certain passages for clarification. But more than this, I hope they can be catalysts for happiness in your life and serve you on your own journey.

You're only as good as your word.

Always do the best you can in everything you do.

Respect everyone.

Be proud of your heritage.

Good news travels far, but bad news travels farther.

The two most important things you have in life are your integrity and your reputation. They will follow you everywhere.

Perseverance and patience are keys to rehabilitation.

Living as your "authentic self" is the most beautiful feeling in the world.

Everyone has an ego, but it's the level of control ego has that will determine if we have a positive or negative ego.

Our ego never stops trying to control how we react.

Life is short—surround yourself with individuals who make you happy.

Always request extra napkins (X always did it, so it must be right).

If it sounds too good to be true, it probably is.

When in doubt, always go with your "gut."

Unlimited patience yields immediate results. (Wayne Dyer)

Faith is the ability to see the invisible and believe in the impossible.

So, to the friend who is reading this book, I'd like to ask you a question:

"What have you learned about yourself lately?"

You don't have to answer right away. The joy is in the exploration, so take your time and explore *yourself.* I truly hope your answer is as beneficial to you as my self-discovery has been for me.

I wish you and yours the best in life and . . .

Namaste *

Dr. Michael Prazich

* **Namaste**, Namaste, pronounced "na-ma-stay," is both a Hindi and a Nepali word. It is said in India and Nepal as a salutation, just as we would say "hello" or "goodbye" in the United Sates. I use it both as a salutation and in parting with the same meaning: "I honor the place in you which is of love, truth, light, and peace."

About the Author

Michael spends most of the year in Scottsdale, Arizona, and four months in the summer on a lake in Minnesota. He keeps busy with Booker and his two companies: Transition Resources, Inc., a nationally recognized dental transition firm active in brokering sales of dental practices, and Perfect Loop Coaching, LLC, his coaching practice. He is also the author of *A Stroke Patient's Own Story—A Personal Guide for Rehabilitation.*

Both Michael and Booker treasure their drive to and from Arizona and try to take a different route each trip. If Michael is the

Lone Ranger, Booker is his Kemo Sabe—they're usually together. His passions include fly-fishing, fresh water fishing and golfing, and he is an avid pistol shooter and an NRA Certified Pistol Instructor.

He can be reached at bookernmike@gmail.com.

88002741R00108

Made in the USA
Lexington, KY
05 May 2018